HOLIDAY CRUISING ON THE BROADS AND FENS

Other books by Lewis Edwards

INLAND WATERWAYS OF GREAT BRITAIN AND IRELAND
(Vols 1 and 2)

Uniform with this book

HOLIDAY CRUISING ON INLAND WATERWAYS
by Charles Hadfield and Michael Streat

HOLIDAY CRUISING ON THE THAMES
by E. and P. W. Ball

HOLIDAY CRUISING IN IRELAND
by P. J. G. Ransom

In preparation

HOLIDAY CRUISING IN FRANCE
by Gerard Grenville-Morgan

HOLIDAY CRUISING ON THE BROADS AND FENS

by

LEWIS EDWARDS

with plates, text illustrations and
Stanford's *Norfolk Broads and Rivers* map with
inset of the Fens

DAVID & CHARLES : NEWTON ABBOT

ISBN 0 7153 5511 3

The author has done his best to make sure that the information given in this book was correct when it went to press, but cannot hold himself responsible for the consequences of any mistakes

Set in 11 on 13 point Plantin
and printed in Great Britain
by W. J. Holman Limited Dawlish
for David & Charles (Publishers) Limited
South Devon House Newton Abbot Devon

Contents

List of Illustrations

PLATES

MAPS AND TEXT ILLUSTRATIONS

This book is dedicated to my wife Patricia whose nocturnal labours have made it possible, and to my son John for enabling me to see East Anglia through new eyes

Preface

In this book I have not tried to duplicate all the information that is available from many popular publications, and the hire agencies give valuable booklets out to all their clients. Instead, I have tried to give some information on those many topics that have been raised by so many people over the years with organisations with which I have been connected.

For the general background to hire cruising this book should be read in conjunction with *Holiday Cruising on Inland Waterways* by Charles Hadfield and Michael Streat, a mine of general information to the beginner and the old hand.

The Broads, were one of the first cruising areas for the holidaymaker in these islands, and facilities are more highly developed there than anywhere else. The nearby Fens provide a remarkable contrast, and yet in spite of the enormous pressures on the area Broadland has survived, largely due to the fact that once the boats withdraw for their winter's sleep the other Broadland can reappear. Hire boats can be obtained all over Britain now, but the real menace to the Broads and Fens will be for more pressure to be applied for shore developments. The country park idea is a form of urbanisation that would be unsuitable for the Fens and Broads in many cases. The pattern is familiar—cars park on the river bank, and after much damage to the surface there is pressure for hard standings to be put down. Car park attendants arrive; toilets have to be installed. Along come mobile fish and chip vans, ice cream vendors, and soon the lonely river bank has become a miniature Blackpool. All over the waterways in East Anglia these pressures are building up, and must be resisted. Let us open up more waterways, make the visitor go afloat and keep certain opened up waterways for sailing craft only. We should concentrate on getting people afloat, and not try to guide them into chalets and shacks on the shore. In the Fens the delightful section of the river from St Neots to St Ives is bound to have pressure put on it, and the remedy is to open up other attractive sections. Similarly, on the Broads the constant harping on the southern rivers will not affect many holidaymakers. The enthusiast will love the Yare and Waveney, but many come for the Broads, and as most of the broads are on the northern rivers they will make for the Bure as soon as they arrive. On the Ouse the locks to Bedford are being rebuilt, and the Middle Level is being looked to as a means of getting to the lovely Nene. Similarly, in Broadland we should be looking to opening the North Walsham Canal and opening up the branches to Meeting Hill and East Ruston. There is indeed much to be done. In other directions, re-education of the public can do untold good and the work of the Norfolk Naturalist Trust in showing visitors what goes on behind the wind in the reeds is of immense value. Bearing in mind the intense urban pressures building up in these islands it is wonderful what we have left in East Anglia. Constant vigilance is necessary, and I urge all to support organisations of 'Light' as Dr Joad called them, referring to bodies for protecting the countryside and waterways.

If you own your own boat, you will doubtless bring your dinghy to explore the little channels, shallow broads and lagoons. Possibly you only own a dinghy but not a cruiser; well, bring it along, but tell the hire agency so that they may make the necessary arrangements for you. If a private owner, may I urge you to join a club, and you will experience great friendship, hospitality and kindness when cruising on strange waters?

Please respect speed limits and keep down your wash. There is no hurry when afloat. Always take care. In particular, do respect that older river user, the fisherman. Boatmen and fishermen have got together on the canals in many places, but mutual understanding is necessary. The Charter for river users issued to all boats that register on the Great Ouse contains much commonsense. Boats should take care near fishing matches and fishermen should try and be seen, as so often they are hidden in the reeds and the boats cannot take evading action.

Happy cruising and a fair wind.

LEWIS A. EDWARDS

Ashtead,
Surrey.

CHAPTER ONE

The Broads, Introduction and Background

Almost since the dawn of history the Norfolk and Suffolk rivers with their broads have been something without parallel in Britain. Even now, with the tremendous pressures which have been imposed upon the area, so much of the old character remains to be found that Broadland is still sought after as a place for a holiday, nature study, bird watching or practically any open air pursuit you care to name. What are the Broads? They are a series of shallow lagoons which lie in north-east Norfolk, with the exception of Oulton Broad which spills over into Suffolk. They lie mainly in a triangle which has at its three points Norwich, Happisburgh and Kessingland in Suffolk. It is an area with a strong regional identity and a wealth of literature. Three very early books written before the turn of the century by Dutt, Davies and Suffling (see p. 135) are still read with interest today. Pleasure cruising began towards the end of the last century, and considerable changes have taken place in the region.

What is it that gives this area such an attraction? Basically, it is because it is so different from any other part of Britain, and those on holiday appreciate the complete change of scene. The Broads are a tidal inlet of the sea; a good deal of the water is brackish and this attracts certain wild life to the area which is not often seen so far inland. Detractors always try to dismiss the Broads as flat, with rivers winding their way through reed beds, but the many families and friends of the area who go year after year know differently. Just moor your boat in a lonely dyke and in a very short time you will see more wild life than in practically any part of this country. Certainly in East Anglia when cruising an open broad you can see the sky in its full majesty for the first time, and the tang of the east coast breezes makes one remarkably hungry. It was no idle boast that the humble little resort of Skegness made for many years in its claim about the bracing air of the east coast.

The region has changed its function in the last half century. It is much less concerned with navigation and trading, and much more with recreation and nature study. The general waterway authority for the region is the Yarmouth Port and Haven Commissioners, and under their jurisdiction the management is carried on by the Rivers Yare, Bure and Waveney Commissioners. Hence the frequent use of the term 'The Commissioners'. Whereas up to the beginning of the last war the traditional wherry (the local sailing barge) was seen trading on the rivers, it has all but disappeared apart from a mere handful of those converted for pleasure cruising and, of course, the famous *Albion*. *Albion,* lovingly restored by the Norfolk Wherry Trust, is normally based at the private mooring at Horning Rectory; she does give a very clear idea of a trading wherry under sail, with perhaps the small exception that most wherries were clinker built and the *Albion* is not. Some of the wherries which survived from the days of sail and were motorised did ply the Broads carrying sugar beet, but now this traffic has also ceased and the beet is carried in lorries, in many cases through towns and villages which could well do without the traffic.

The mills on the Broads give the area a distinctive quality, akin more to Holland than England as it is generally known. Many were wind pumps used for draining the low lying dykes, and in days gone by holidaymakers used to avoid mooring for the night near these wind pumps because of the creaking and groaning noises which echoed over the marshes. The mills are now silent, some decayed, but happily some restored to their original glory by various bodies working together.

A good many of the village buildings are thatched with Norfolk reed thatch; properly tended, reed thatch has a long life. Thatching is a thriving industry, and you will still see piles of reeds in certain places on the Broads waiting to be taken away, in some cases for export. Some reeds have even been exported to Ireland for restoring cabins for the use of the holiday-makers.

The churches are a dominant feature of parts of the Broadland scene. Many Norfolk churches have round towers; there is some evidence to show that these towers were constructed before the churches, and it is thought that the round towers were originally built as works of defence in an area which was subject to a number of invasions. There does seem to be a connection between the round towered churches of Norfolk and those of Ireland, but no one as yet seems to have made a particular study of this subject.

The Broads villages present as a common feature something that is generally lacking elsewhere—the village landing stage. On canals and rivers, goods were often landed at canal company wharves or privately owned quays, works basins etc. In bigger towns and cities there is usually a public wharf or hard, but in Broadland most villages have their own landing place, or staithe as it is called locally.

From earliest days the rivers in Broadland were the only highways. During the centuries of invasion after the withdrawal of the Roman legions, the first essential for any sea-rover's settlement was a 'staeth', Anglo-Saxon for landing place. From the sixth century onwards, Broadland villages largely developed round the parish staithe. It was the essential link with the outside world, and villagers had free use of it for commerce and recreation.

Many staithes are still usable, and the main problem is the

cost of upkeep, often a heavy burden on a small parish. Please give a donation towards this when you use a staithe. The hire agencies have assisted considerably in the past, but the practice now seems to tend towards covering maintenance costs more centrally. Moorings which are maintained by one or other of the agencies in key positions are not restricted to that agency's boats. Blake's efforts at Ranworth are appreciated by all, just as were Hoseasons' at Catfield Wood End. In both these cases the Commissioners have rendered considerable assistance. Ownership of Dilham staithe is vested in the East Anglian Waterways' Association, but it will probably be leased to the Commissioners for the benefit of the parish and visitors, irrespective of which club or association the waterborne traveller is a member. This should be a pattern for future development. The use of some of the more lonely staithes is particularly commended to the reader. If one is not a keen naturalist, a pair of binoculars and a little patience will soon make you one.

A list of most parish staithes can be found in *Inland Waterways of Great Britain and Ireland,* Volume I, Norfolk Broads section (Imray Norie Laurie and Wilson, 1972). Mr Vincent Ellis, Clerk to the East Suffolk and Norfolk River Authority, has offered, providing suitable notice is given, to show various documents in his possession to serious students of the subject of parish staithes. Up to date information can usually be obtained from the Chief Inspector of the Yare, Bure and Waveney Commissioners, again providing notice is given.

Broadland has one of the widest varieties of flora and fauna to be studied at close quarters in the British Isles. Probably the first wild mammal the hirer will see is the coypu, a great swimmer, and usually a surprise to those seeing it for the first time as it is quite the largest 'rat' he will see anywhere in the United Kingdom. The coypu were brought to East Anglia from South America for their fur, but a number escaped from the fur farms and set up colonies under the reed beds. Then there is the otter, a great lover of eels; many are to be found in the more lonely parts of Broadland. The nest, or more accurately 'the holt', is in bunches of reeds, unlike their usual habitat of tree roots. The greatest fisherman of the Broads, however, is the heron, who is a passionately devoted eel catcher. Wherever you moor your boat in the lonely parts of Broadland, you will hear numerous plops in the water caused by the water vole, a delightful little animal with an attractive round face, different from the rat in almost every way, but similar in size. It is a pest in the sense that it tunnels into banks and undermines them.

Amongst the wild fowl there is the shoveller, famous for the shape of its bill; the marsh harrier, which varies so much in colour and markings that each seems to be different, and, although it arrived late to breed on the Broads, the Garganey teal, common from Lincolnshire to Kent, now breeds here. Moorhens are to be seen everywhere; very like the coot, they nest in the reeds. The snipe is variable in its habits. Not many breed here, but with their markedly irregular flight numbers arrive as the leaves begin to turn. The bittern is probably the bird which most reminds one of the Broads. Its colouring is very like the reed beds where it nests. Some years ago the bittern was absent from the Broads, but it returned first to Barton, and now its familiar booming note is heard over most parts of the Broads. The return of the bittern is a story in itself. The coot is everywhere, a friendly and delightful bird, which in winter time tends to move towards the lower reaches of the rivers and the edges of the sea.

In all seasons of the year the bird life is magnificent: take your binoculars with you, be patient and seek a quiet mooring. For further information see the section on bird life by Emma L. Turner in the classic *The Norfolk Broads* by W. A. Dutt. This can be found in many libraries, and is not difficult to pick up in second-hand book shops.

In 1965 the Nature Conservancy issued a report on Broadland, which any interested person should study. Dr E. A. Ellis, long-standing contributor to *The Eastern Daily Press,* gives a good introduction to the natural life of the area in *The Broads.* He mentions water species of charophytes and the stagshorn weed (*Naias marina*), unknown elsewhere in these islands; water soldier and cowbane, and massive ranks of the tall marsh sowthistle along miles of riverside; the fen orchid and round-leaved wintergreen in the mossy fens and the great spearwort raising its yellow heads between the reeds. He writes of little fungi which thrive in the humid shelter of tall marsh vegetation; of the remarkable range of planktonic animals in the saline regions including many curiously specialised crustaceans, and freshwater polyzoa; molluscs in the more calcareous regions and brackish-water species on the lower riverside reaches.

Among the insects, Dr Ellis mentions the British swallowtail butterfly, surviving in abundance nowhere else, and two dragonflies which are restricted to this region; many rare and local moths among the reed beds, especially the wainscots; and a new British footman, *Pelosia obtusa,* found in 1961 near one of the broads. He says that almost all its specialised insects and other invertebrates of the ancient fenland now drained, as well as its plants, are represented in the broadland region.

The Norwich Society River Group (Hon Sec Mrs G. Reading), Holly Lodge, Telegraph Lane, West Thorpe, Norwich (NRO 373), issue a detailed publication on the waterways of Norwich giving unusual information.

J. Wentworth Day's book *Portrait of the Broads* is another good introduction to this area. The Norfolk Naturalists' Trust, founded in 1926, shares with the National Trust the management of coastal reserves at Blakeney Point—1,335 acres; Scolt Head Island—1,821 acres; and Arnold's Marsh at Clay—29 acres. There is inevitably bound to be some conflict of interest between these various reserves and other concerns, but all naturalists cannot be keen boatmen and vice versa. The Wetland Sites of interest to the Nature Conservancy on the Broads and nearby (see also Chapter 5—*Closed Broads and Closed Navigations*) are as follows:

Site	*County*	*Map Ref.*	*Acreage*
Alderfen Broad	Norfolk	TG355195	47
Daylham Fishponds	Suffolk	TM104531	c.40
Barton Broad	Norfolk	TG358215	562
Bosmere	Suffolk	TM097547	c.10
Bure Marshes	Norfolk	TG335169	1019
Burgh Common	Norfolk	TG445127	141
Burntfen Broad	Norfolk	TG339186	86
Calthorpe Broad	Norfolk	TG412258	111
Decoypond Wood, Purdis Farm	Suffolk	TM208433	42
The Doles	Norfolk	TG390135	255
Flixton Decoy	Suffolk	TM512955	c.50
Fritton Decoy	Suffolk	TG483005	420
Hardley Floods	Norfolk	TM380997	120
Hickling Broad	Norfolk	TG420215	1204
Holkham Lake	Norfolk	TG883435	110
Horsey Mere	Norfolk	TG450222	500
Lenwade Pools	Norfolk	TG108186	c.100
Martham Broad	Norfolk	TG458203	189
Redgrave and Lopham Fens	Suffolk	TM050795	303
Sea Mere, Hingham	Norfolk	TH035012	98
Surlingham and Rockland Broads	Norfolk	TG326065	740
Sutton Broad	Norfolk	TG356235	421
Sparham Pools	Norfolk	TG063186	c.25
Sudbury Meadows	Suffolk	TL8641 & TL8740	c.300

The Hickling Water Trail, which runs through the Nature Reserve established at Hickling Broad by the late Lord Desborough, leads you to where many uncommon plants and insects can be seen. The water in Hickling Broad is only slightly brackish, due probably to the proximity of the North Sea, just over three miles away.

On a trip round the Hickling Water Trail visitors will be shown the difference between reeds and sedge, the latter being cut in the summer, whereas the reeds are always harvested for thatching early in the year. Sedge will be seen on thatched roofs as it is an ideal capping material. Reeds are a popular background for bearded tits and bitterns.

There are numerous plants providing food for the extensive butterfly population and the quantities of dragon-flies. Hickling has also a number of hawk moth, as well as some of the rarer varieties. You will also notice that some of the sedge beds have not been cut for some years; these provide a nesting place for a number of rare birds.

Usually on a trip around the trail you will see two birds fond of this habitat, the reed bunting and the sedge warbler. It is interesting also to search for the peat areas where there is little sedge or reed. These bald patches are caused by coypus, which have done a lot of damage to sedge beds, and the Ministry of Agriculture, Fisheries & Food have for some years conducted a campaign to control them. In the twelve months period 1 April 1969 to 31 March 1970, 967 coypus were destroyed in Norfolk and Suffolk.

On the trail the Wagonhill Plantation gives a very fine cross section of trees. Oak is the most popular, and there are some ancient alders. This Broadland plantation is markedly different with its bracken on the ground and few shrubs from the usual English plantation with its understorey of hazel and other shrubs. At Wagonhill the heron are reappearing after the disastrous loss of so many during the bitter winter of 1962-63.

In winter (and a visit out of season is strongly recommended) Hickling is the place to see large numbers of wildfowl in the shallow bay near Higham Corner.

These can only be a few notes on a wide subject. The newcomer to Broadland could well visit his public library on his return home, as most have a number of the better-known books on this area.

In his *Portrait of the Broads,* J. Wentworth Day lists 108

birds that were reported as seen by a member of the Norfolk Naturalists' Trust and his two sons between 22 and 26 April 1964. The animal population is, of course, much less. Foxes are not very common, but they are increasing. Old brock, the badger, is a most uncommon animal here, and the only one ever seen by the author was in the upper reaches of the North Walsham Canal. The coypu has already been referred to. The visitor should remember that he will not attack you unless you attempt to attack him. There are stoats and weasels, hares and rabbits, plenty of moles in the marshland, and an abundance of hedgehogs. Rats abound in varieties, and it is interesting to distinguish between the different varieties of water rats and voles which you can see at lonely moorings.

More than anything else it is the vegetation and wild life that makes Broadland a place to which the visitor continually returns. If you are going in for bird watching you should do it alone or in very small groups.

In conclusion, please help to preserve the area by taking great care that you avoid damaging banks, shoreline vegetation and marshland. Do not disturb nesting birds, and avoid shallow water where fish may spawn. Make sure that you use the litter baskets provided at recognized mooring and parking places and yacht stations. Never leave any litter about on land or water; take it with you for suitable disposal or bury it good and deep. Be particularly careful how you dispose of plastic, cellophane, and other indestructible materials; they must never be left about, as they can kill or maim wildlife. Do not pollute the water or banks in any way, and use public lavatories on shore whenever you can. Remember all the land adjoining the water belongs to someone and respect this ownership. Do not trespass.

Fishing has always been a great Broadland pursuit, and when the boats have seen the last of the holidaymaker the long moorings at many of the popular inns have a change of visitor and row upon row of anglers, many from the industrial Midlands and North, can be found coarse fishing for bream, roach, rudd and perch. If you are lucky, there are record pike to be taken. By enjoying Broadland in the summer you will obviously have avoided some of the gregarious things always to be found in a holiday area. But out of the holiday season you will find Broadland an even better place, and you will have an opportunity to obtain advice from and conversation with some of the real marshmen whose tales round the fires of the village inns will always linger in the memory. The author remembers on a November night sitting with the late Alf Amis and some of those characters who are now legendary at the Pleasure Boat and reflecting that the faces lit by the firelight clearly showed their Norse origin.

The Broads have not been designated a National Park. The story is too long to go into here, but turned partly on the inherent character of the water and partly on the lack of local support when the proposal was under discussion between 1955 and 1961. The Bowes Committee set up in 1956 reported on the Broads, though they were not generally included in the national waterway system, but a detached section. They are under the general authority of the Yarmouth Port and Haven Commissioners, which body was suggested for reconstitution (also a recommendation of the Bowes Committee) on a more modern and representative basis. The report was published in 1958 and did not suggest amalgamating the River Authority and Commissioners.

The Nature Conservancy did a draft survey of the Broads which was published early in 1963, and the *Report on Broadland* published by the Nature Conservancy in London in July 1965 is an important and interesting document. Following this report a Broads Consortium Committee was set up consisting of the Norfolk County Council, the East Suffolk and Norfolk River Authority, the Great Yarmouth Port and Haven Commissioners, and the East Suffolk County Council. This report is of great interest to everyone interested in the Broads and a copy can be obtained at £1.60 from the Planning Department, County Hall, Norwich, NOR 47A. This report was approved by the four authorities, subject to certain reservations concerning the Yarmouth Barrage and the new Authority. Waterway campaigners should make certain they obtain from the Commissioners a copy of their Minority Report which challenges the Consortium's recommendation for amalgamating the Commissioners and the River Authority. This suggestion has caused a great furore in the area and appears to have no support whatever from the tollpayers and the subtle implication behind the takeover bid could have serious repercussions on waterway management all over the country. The serious enthusiast will doubtless make further enquiries, and this perhaps could be the subject of another book! The evidence for the proposed takeover appears very scanty, and if the precedent established elsewhere is anything to go by, the cruising waterman could be in for a very thin time.

The Broads have long been frequented by anglers and naturalists, indeed for several hundred years. In this century modern holiday trade has developed, and proved enormously popular. The facilities here are more highly developed than anywhere else. In fact, visitors are attracted from abroad as boat hire facilities in some continental countries are almost unknown, ironically enough because in Europe the inland waterways carry heavy commercial traffic. In a holiday season from March to October it is thought that something like 350,000 people visit the area, and there are over 10,000 boats, although fortunately not all of them are out at the same time. The anglers total over 60,000. This undoubtedly has led to congestion in certain well defined areas, but sensible holiday planning even at peak holiday periods can be most rewarding. Facilities for food and fuel are highly organised, and with the exception of Windermere, it is the only inland area where cruising yachts can be hired. There are very well developed holiday centres with chalets with day boat facilities, and there are many houseboats to be hired, almost unknown elsewhere. Some people decry houseboats, but they form an excellent start for those unused to waterway holidays, and provide plenty of room for a mother to look after young children. Most houseboats are hired out with a boat or launch, and some of the more sensitive appreciation of Broadland has come from those who have explored the lesser known dykes, accessible only to the rowing boat, from their houseboat. Children can be introduced to water life this way. It is important to respect quiet and privacy, to keep down transistor volume, to avoid songs and revelry close to other moorings, and to be scrupulous in leaving no litter or refuse anywhere.

Hire cruisers form the bulk of the Broadland holiday craft, and the variety defies description. There is a lot to be said for visiting a yard during the off season and looking for oneself. It is so often the case that the Broads give folk the first taste of a waterway holiday, and first impressions generally linger longest.

If you have never had a holiday afloat, Broadland is the place to go, and if you are a complete novice you will often find the friendly yard staff will be most helpful, though it is best to keep clear of the busy hours of turn round of the boats at weekends. You will get the most fun out of it if you read up as much as you can about boat life and the Broadland background beforehand. You will find probably the greatest mixture of humanity to be seen anywhere, and you never know whom you will meet. The author has vivid memories of an occasion where a large 8-berth cruiser with a most garishly dressed crew wearing hats with slogans approached some yacht at an exclusive yacht club. The comments quickly changed when it was seen that the cruiser was going to the rescue of a yacht in trouble, and in spite of the unseasonable bad weather with a force 6 gale blowing, the yacht was brought in; the cruiser was moored up in professional fashion and cordial thanks expressed by the rescued. The hire cruiser skipper, sensing the thoughts of the onlookers, explained that it was all in a day's work as his job was a tugmaster on the Trent!

The following is a list of the main broads and lakes: these

have been taken from the Eastern Sports Council's publication *A Regional Strategy for Water Recreation 1971.* There are fishing and boating facilities on some of the landlocked broads, and access is possible in some cases for members of naturalists' organisations and fishing clubs. The enthusiast who takes the trouble to make inquiries locally may be led on an exploration of an unknown corner of Broadland. In spite of the reduction in area of many of the broads, the work of the Commissioners, since the war in particular, has made some of the broads in better condition than they were fifty years ago.

Navigation Broads and Lakes
(all figures are approximate)

Norfolk

Barton Broad (162 acres—originally 284 acres)
Bridge Broad (10 acres)
Heigham Sound (65 acres but only a navigation channel open. Originally 111 acres)
Hickling Broad (302 acres—originally 485 acres)
Horsey Mere (65 acres—originally 109 acres)
Hoveton Little Broad (47 acres)
Malthouse Broad (22 acres)
Martham Broad (37 acres but only a navigation channel open. Originally 115 acres)
Rockland Broad (27 acres—originally 87 acres)
Salhouse Great Broad (21 acres)
South Walsham Broad (Inner and Outer) (38 acres—originally 69 acres)
Surlingham & Bargate Broad (8 acres but only a navigation channel open. Originally 72 acres)
Sutton Broad (navigation channels only. Remaining 190 acres extinct)
Womack Water (navigation channel only)
Wroxham Broad (69 acres—originally 80 acres)
Breydon Water (2,000 acres)

E. Suffolk
Oulton Broad (84 acres)

The boat hirer will obtain from the hiring agency a copy of the rules of the river incorporated in a handbook, and the private owner will obtain these in the bye-laws when he registers his boat with the Yarmouth Port and Haven Commissioners. Rule 30 in the International Regulations lays down that special rules or local bye-laws take precedence over the International Regulations. The Broads bye-laws are seriously out of date and may well have been revised by the time this book appears in print.

Care should be taken to observe the rules regarding giving way to yachts, and remember that any boat towing a vessel has right of way. Familiarise yourself with the sound signals as laid down and pay particular attention to signals from ships on the Yare which need a deep channel and cannot easily manoeuvre. The signals will give you instructions about their movements and indicate towards which bank you should go. Channels on shallow broads are marked by posts, buoys or leading markers. They are marked all in the same way, the port-hand (left side going upstream) markings are painted red, the starboard-hand are black with a white top. There are special markings on Hickling and Horsey which are given in the latest handbooks. Care should be taken with a number of the sailing clubs where there are beginners as well as experienced yachtsmen, and in some cases helmsmen appear to be unaware that large cruisers needing deep water cannot invariably give way to sail. The latter statement is often made for convenience, but yachtsmen should always take care when in the vicinity of power craft that are unable to leave the narrow navigation channel. Take great care not to leave the marked channel, otherwise you will go aground. The speed limit must be carefully observed, and this is enforced by timed speed checks. Hire firms do not permit navigation after dark, or below South

Town Bridge in Great Yarmouth, nor through Mutford Lock into Lake Lothing.

There are plenty of free moorings in the open countryside of Broadland, and apart from the weekends you can always moor free of charge in the boatyard flying the same agency flag as yours. However, in spite of the popular business rivalry, you can in fact moor in any yard you like if certain courtesies are observed. Sometimes a fee is asked for upkeep purposes, or a donation towards staithe maintenance. Blakes yards charge a mooring fee as a general rule to all craft not in the Blakes organisation. Hoseason on the other hand offer free moorings on weekdays, subject to space being available, to any craft on the Broads. The position varies from yard to yard.

There are excellent yacht stations at Great Yarmouth, Oulton Broad, Norwich and Beccles, and numerous other popular moorings at parish staithes in villages.

Bridges in Broadland need care. There is a warning board on low Broads bridges displayed by the arch that is to be used for navigation. The Commissioners have placed gauges at some bridges which give you the headroom as you approach the bridge. It is certainly generally advisable to use a pilot at Potter Heigham. Notice boards west of the bridge tell you where you can find pilots for Blakes' and Hoseason's boats.The Red Whale pilot is at Richardson's yard by the bridge. Private owners desiring pilotage make their own arrangements with a pilot. If you are in doubt, moor up and ask at the boatyard. The hirer should note his headroom figure on a plate in his cockpit. Make certain there is ample clearance, lower your windscreens, canopies and masts. In the case of swing bridges wave an easily identified object so that the bridge man can prepare to open the bridge when he is able to do so. The greatest hazard on the Broads does not in fact exist unless you are exceptionally careless, and that is navigating through Great Yarmouth. Study the river distances from the map and check on local tide tables, then work out in advance your arrival time at Yarmouth. If in doubt check at a boatyard on the way down.

The best time to navigate is when the ebb and flow of the tide has ceased, and this is usually 1½ hours after low water. Before this time the ebb can be very fast. There are special instructions for yachtsmen, but if you are a beginner under sail take extra care and make certain you obtain expert advice before going round. Great care should be taken across Breydon, and under no circumstances try and take short cuts. You will invariably end up on the 'putty'.

CHAPTER TWO

Cruising the Northern Rivers

The Northern rivers are the Bure, Ant and Thurne

River Bure

The longest is the Bure which rises at the little town of Melton Constable, once a miniature Crewe for the Midland & Great Northern Railway. As far as Coltishall it is a very clear stream, popular with anglers. Here the river becomes a navigation, and a boat slide has been installed at the old lock (inoperable) to enable light craft to go upstream towards Buxton Lammas. There are two arms to the upper reaches, the southern one leading to the site of Horstead Mill which was burnt down in 1963. These upper arms are shallows and do not always have enough depth for cruisers. A popular mooring is the Rising Sun, the first of the Bureside inns; the King's Head is nearby, and the usual facilities by the river. From the Rising Sun to the Anchor Hotel is Coltishall Common, a popular mooring particularly for those with families, and below the Anchor Hotel, which has a very long section of well quay-headed moorings, is the boatyard of Clifford Allen, which is claimed to be the oldest on the Broads. Allen's boats can be found far and wide; the author has been aboard one on the northern Shannon.

The next village is Belaugh, and this pretty place by the river nails the lie that Broadland is flat everywhere. Wroxham is the next place downstream, a distance of nearly five miles from Coltishall. The name Wroxham is applied incorrectly but generally to both sides of the river, although strictly speaking the town on the northern side is Hoveton St John. Wroxham took up hiring out yachts before the turn of the century and is now a major hiring centre. Full details of the yards both here and elsewhere may be obtained from the four hiring agencies which will be referred to later. Apart from small town shops there is, of course, Roy's, which used to call itself the largest village store in the world and once even owned the public conveniences. Facilities are excellent and full particulars are in the booklets issued to every hire cruiser visitor. Wroxham has an extremely well run fleet of day launches operated in connection with excursions from all over Britain by Broads Tours under the direction of C. A. Hannaford, a great Broadsman and a very fine painter; an art gallery of his works in his dining rooms is well worth a visit.

The King's Head Hotel, the Horseshoes, the Castle Inn and the Bure Court Hotel all have moorings for visitors, and the Broads Hotel and Club nearby is a useful part of call. On leaving Wroxham great care should be taken at the road bridge which, although not quite such a terror as Potter Heigham, needs special care as large pleasure boats use this section of the river.

Before one leaves Wroxham, if it is the third Sunday in the month, a visit should be made to Barton House Railway. This is open from April to October from 2.30 to 5.30 pm, with special openings by prior arrangement. Barton House is situated at the end of The Avenue on the south side of the river. Here is a live steam miniature railway which carries passengers, but unlike any other venture of its kind, it has full sized signals and signalling equipment operated from a signal box completely restored to working order. This originally stood at Honing Station near the North Walsham Canal.

The section from Wroxham to Horning Ferry is five and a half miles. It is well wooded and passes Wroxham Broad, a famous yachting centre, the smaller Salhouse Great Broad, and

Hoveton Little Broad which is open for most of the summer cruising season, but closed in the winter. The latter broad is sometimes called Black Horse Broad after the inn on the road running on the hill on the northern bank. There does not appear to be access to the inn from the water.

By far the most interesting event in recent years has been the opening of the Hoveton Great Broad Nature Trail by agreement with the owner, Mr T. C. R. Blofield. The Trail is reached from a mooring located on the north bank of the river, 380yd upstream of the entrance to Salhouse Broad. There is no charge for admission and during the cruising season the Trail is open from 10 am to 5.30 pm in the week and 2 pm to 5.30 pm on Sundays. It is closed on Saturdays. The Trail is over half a mile long and foundations have been laid throughout its length to provide a suitable walking route, but great care should be taken to keep to the path which is mainly constructed from old railway sleepers. In this Trail you will see a section of unreclaimed fen, marsh fern, mosses and lichens, a miniature turf pond, young alders, a section of the broad which is a bird haunt and, amongst many other things, the Norfolk reed.

The old route for wherries was through a dyke near Southgates Boatyard, across Hoveton Little Broad, through the section now closed as a nature reserve at the western end, and then through a further short cut made through Hoveton Great Broad and Hudson's Bay. Near the closed Decoy Broad on the north bank is Dydler's Mill. This is a studio conversion of an old mill. The name Dydler relates to a long pole fitted with a scoop of wire mesh which was used for clearing out dykes and recovering articles that had been dropped into the water. The expression 'dydle it out' is still used regularly.

Horning is considered by many to be the prettiest village on the Broads, although naturally there are other claimants. Great care should be taken on the bend of the river by the Swan Inn as there are frequently yachting activities by the Horning Sailing Club. The speed limit through Horning is rigorously imposed because of the number of moored craft. There are three inns, the Swan on the corner; the New Inn, oldest in the village with good moorings, and the Ferry. The Ferry was destroyed by enemy action during the war with serious loss of life, and in recent years the thatched roof caught fire, badly damaging the rebuilt inn. It has risen again for the third time and is a very popular port of call with excellent moorings for the visitor. Alas, Horning ferry no longer operates. In the village there is also the Petersfield Hotel, and numerous boat-yards. Some of the gardens are a joy to the eye. There are few moorings below Horning, but the enthusiast will spot on many occasions the wherry *Albion,* already referred to. Horning Church has excellent moorings for Morning Service, even when *Albion* is 'at home'.

Ranworth Dyke very soon appears, leading to Malthouse Broad. The adjoining Ranworth Broad is a bird sanctuary and is closed to navigation. Ranworth Dyke is narrow, but deep, and Malthouse Broad has been much improved by dredging in recent years. The Commissioners as an experiment dredged deep holes all over the broad: allowing for the ebb and flow of the tide it was hoped that the holes would fill up, slowly increasing the depth of the whole broad, and this seems to have happened. The Maltsters is the inn at Ranworth staithe, the latter managed by Blakes for all visitors, and the excellent facilities are enhanced by the very fine church on the hill overlooking the broads. Here depicted are the twelve Apostles on one of the very best rood screens in England. This has been restored to its former glory and visitors should make a point of seeing the antiphonary which was written by the monks of the nearby Langley Abbey.

On returning to the main river going downstream you pass Horning Hall, of great age and interest. Ant mouth is shortly reached, $12\frac{1}{4}$ miles from Coltishall. Opposite Ant mouth is the old course of the River Bure which leads into Fleet Dyke, which in turn leads into South Walsham Broad. This dyke from Ant mouth is not navigable, and the only route into the broad is via South Walsham dyke. The inner and outer broads have been extensively dredged in recent years by the Commissioners, and these two sections of water probably form the most unspoilt of any of the broads. There are boatyard facilities and stores obtainable in the village. The inner broad is particularly useful for enthusiasts and bird watchers. The rowing dinghy is much to be preferred for such a trip.

Returning to the main river and going downstream, the ruins of St Benet's Abbey soon come into view on the north bank. The abbey has had a long history. It was attacked by people from Ludham during the Peasants' Revolt in 1381. Now on the first Sunday in every August there is a service held at which the Bishop of Norwich officiates as the Abbot of St Benet's, and preaches to a large gathering.

At Thurne mouth, fifteen miles from Coltishall, there is a junction with the river Thurne, the Bure continuing towards the sea. On the route to Great Yarmouth Upton Dyke leads to the village of Upton Green where the local inn is The Cock. At Acle Bridge there is the Bridge Hotel and two boatyards. A short distance downstream is Acle Dyke, leading part of the way to Acle village where there are three more inns. The river now runs through very flat Fen type country past Muck Fleet which unfortunately is not navigable, but which leads to the landlocked, but very lovely Filby, Ormesby and Rollesby broads.

The section now being entered needs considerable care as the effect of the tides becomes greater, and if there is the slightest doubt in the mind of the navigator he should take advice from the nearest boatyard. This is the area which has been changed over many years by land drainage, symbolised by the very fine private mills lovingly restored by local bodies. There are a number of mills to be seen on the Bure and tributaries in various states of preservation and dereliction, and the campaign to restore these to their previous glory is a project which should have the support of all those who can help.

Stokesby is the last habitation to be seen before Yarmouth,

Page 33 (*above*) Change-over day in Herbert Woods' yard at Potter Heigham, River Thurne; (*below*) Barton Broad. A popular method of cruising is to hire a cruiser and also a sailing dinghy. The cruiser can be moored on the Broad and the crew can sail in the dinghy.

Page 34 (*above*) Catfield Wood End staithe, near Barton Broad. A popular method of cruising is to have a day launch from Loynes of Wroxham, and sleep ashore in one of the many holiday homes; (*below*) Horning Parish staithe, River Bure.

on the north bank. The church is interesting, and just below the village is The Stracey Arms, a good riverside inn on the main road. Before reaching this inn there is Tunstall Dyke, previously a wherry branch line, but now forgotten. In these lower reaches towards Yarmouth the moorings are generally unsatisfactory. Sometimes there is deep water, on other occasions there are shallows on the inside of bends. Mooring is inadvisable after the Stracey Arms until Great Yarmouth is reached. There are a few good places known to the local inhabitants, but a stranger should beware. There is a large yacht station at Great Yarmouth managed by Blakes for the benefit of all; great care should be taken as the river can flow very swiftly at this point. Through navigation from the Bure to the Waveney is not difficult, providing proper care is taken.

River Ant

The two tributaries, the Ant and the Thurne, bring in some delightful water, particularly Barton and Hickling. From the junction of the Ant with the Bure, the countryside is not of interest until one passes the new bridge at Ludham; then it winds round until How Hill, a thatched mansion on the east bank, comes into view. Small wherries can be seen taking away piles of reeds which are cut in the locality. Here is the entrance to Crome's Broad now, alas, severed from the cruising network. Moorings are not difficult on the Ant, but avoid the submerged piles which can be found in the river from Barton downstream; they were the old wooden quay headings put in years ago by the drainage authorities. At Irstead there is a tiny staithe, a delightful but lonely church, and a very narrow section of river about 100yd long with a gravel bottom, which goes into Barton Broad. Barton is somewhat like a distorted triangle with the Irstead end and Neatishead as the base and Barton Common as the apex.

One of the greatest delights on this section of river are the water gardens of How Hill. They cannot be seen from the water, but consist of numerous tiny canals in woodland with magnificent rhododendrons, azaleas and other flowering shrubs. These, one of the loveliest of Britain's water gardens, used to be open to the public on occasions by the previous owner, and the determined enthusiast could well make inquiries from the Norfolk County Council, who now own the property, as details appear to be sparse.

There are several voyages to be made on Barton. Coming up the Ant keeping south of Pleasure Hill island, there is a very pleasant dyke and mooring at Neatishead village with two inns and the usual village appurtenances. There is also an easy mooring at Gay's staithe in a short branch off the bottom of Lime Kiln Dyke. Neatishead Church must have been huge, but only the chancel remains, with a fine old font and pulpit. On the eastern side of the broad above Pleasure Hill island, is the entrance to Catfield Wood End staithe, a lonely mooring which has been restored in recent years with the help of Hoseason's Broadland Agency. Barton Turf is a hamlet on the eastern side at the top of the broad. The church, whose medieval tower stands as a lonely sentinel in the countryside, has several rare possessions and a very fine rood screen, only excelled at Ranworth. Barton is certainly one of the loveliest broads, fringed around its edges with reeds, and the haunt of a wide variety of wild fowl. Horatio Nelson learnt to sail here. Barton is popular with the visitor who likes to hire a cruiser and moor it in the broad with a mud weight and then explore the many inlets and corners of the broad in a dinghy. Mooring in a broad on a still evening, using the mud weight (supplied with all Broads hire boats), is an experience not to be missed, but necessary care should be taken.

Above Barton there are two channels running eastwards; one to Stalham, a small country town with above average shopping facilities, and the other to Sutton, a small village on the Stalham to Potter Heigham road, with a village store and a post office. Sutton Broad has almost grown over, but the channel is a wide one and there is plenty of room to moor at the staithe where there is a country club and hotel. This long, low red brick building was once the old Wherrymans Arms, and that great East Anglian writer, J. Wentworth Day, engagingly speculates in *Marshland Adventure* about the goings on and rough-doings at this sort of smugglers' den. It became the staithe farm for over eighty years; then this delightful corner was brought to life in 1928 by the late Basil Hitching who turned it into a warm, friendly place of relics from the sea and land, and old brass. Although Basil died soon after his retirement in 1961 he is not forgotten in this corner of the Broads, and the club, recently enlarged, caters for larger parties than ever.

From the Ant mouth it is 4½ miles to Irstead, 5¼ miles at the north side of Barton Broad, 6⅝ miles at the junction to Stalham and Sutton, and a total of 8 miles to Wayford Bridge. This section is narrow, but deep and through delightfully wooded country. On the way there is Huntset Mill, the most beautiful mill in Broadland with a magnificent white cap and sails, and its nearby house and garden are in superb order. Much photographed, it still remains a 'must' for the cameraman.

At Wayford Bridge there are boatyards, a store, restaurant and inn. The restaurant is licensed, and is trying hard to raise the gastronomic standards of a district where eating out amongst the local inhabitants is not such an established custom as elsewhere. The restaurant is located in the old Wayford Bridge Hotel, which lost its licence. However, a new inn was created on the other side of the river, Wood Farm, a Free House. The last pint in the old inn was served to the author.

The moorings above Wayford on the west bank are long, wide, well maintained and very popular. It is possible to go on up the main river, which some 150yd above the junction with the route to Dilham is called the North Walsham Canal. The North Walsham Canal is, in fact, a canalised river but in times of high water a small cruiser can go up 2½ miles and turn at the ruins of Honing Lock, but you must keep to the left bank.

This lonely stretch of water is an ideal trip by dinghy, but the branch to East Ruston village is silted up at the present time. The Smallburgh River which leaves the Ant on the west bank runs to Dilham village, a lonely waterway although now open to traffic. There is no mooring before Dilham, where there are some privately owned dykes on the north bank, and although these sometimes offer moorings for a fee, the proper mooring is at the top of the dyke which is quay headed, by Brick Kiln Bridge. The dyke, from the junction with the river to the bridge, is owned by The East Anglian Waterways Association Ltd, whose efforts led to this section of river being reopened, but the Commissioners' bye-laws apply throughout. There is a village inn and stores very close to the mooring, but it is necessary to walk into the next village of Smallburgh, only another half mile, for the post office. The walk is well worth while as there is an excellent inn, the Crown, unspoilt, unaltered and spotlessly clean.

This book is for the enthusiast who tries to look a little further than the average guide book, and Dilham means much to such a person. The reason why Dilham has been the object of attention by enthusiasts is that Sir William Cubitt was born here, the son of a Dilham miller, who canalised and improved rivers, cut canals, did railway engineering and was instrumental in carrying out vast drainage schemes. At Dilham staithe one can reflect that Sir William Cubitt, together with Edward Leader Williams, were the engineers of the mighty navigation works on the River Severn. This is the only staithe on the Broads that has been created by enthusiasts, and donations towards its upkeep will always be gratefully received by the Village Stores. Above the bridge are the remains of the canal to the brickworks which supplied Norwich with many of the bricks for its houses. Bricks were a main cargo for wherries.

Returning to Wayford Bridge, it is interesting to recall that it was indeed Way Ford before the bridge, as dredging contractors have found out. Just north of the bridge are the remains of the ford and submerged road which limit the draught of boats to 3ft. The bridge itself also limits craft wishing to reach the river above; generally it has a headroom of 7ft.

River Thurne

The River Thurne which joins the Bure at Thurne Mouth, is a gateway to more broads. After leaving the junction with the main river, there is a quay-headed short dyke leading to the Lion Inn at Thurne village with a very fine restored wind pump at the entrance. A short distance upstream is Womack Water, which is the remains of the old Womack Broad. This has been well restored in recent years and is not the narrow, difficult channel it used to be. This mooring is very close to Ludham village where is the church of St Catherine with a hammer-beam roof, and one of Norfolk's finest rood screens. Opposite the church is the King's Arms.

Going further upstream Potter Heigham is reached. This bridge is a well-known navigational legend. Take extra care. Potter Heigham is primarily a boat building village. Upstream is the junction with Candle (Kendal) Dyke and the channel northwards through Heigham Sound and White Slea into Hickling. Hickling is a shallow broad, and throughout this section from Candle Dyke it is essential to keep to the marked channel. On leaving Hickling Broad there are two routes, one eastwards across the broad and up Catfield Dyke to Catfield Staithe. This is narrow but has a turning point. Halfway along Catfield Dyke is a branch which leads to Catfield Common Staithe. The dyke is not suitable for craft over 9ft beam. The other equally popular route is to the Pleasure Boat on the north end of the broad. This is some way from Hickling village, although the enthusiast for architecture could well walk there to explore the church, and en route there are several unsophisticated inns. The Pleasure Boat used to be run by the late Alf Amis, one of those legendary Broadsmen some of us were privileged to have met. It was typical of Alf that he never told anyone the room where the Duke of Edinburgh and Prince Charles slept when floods made them take accommodation at the inn.

After crossing Heigham Sound on the north side you arrive at Meadow Dyke, which leads to Horsey Mere, 7 miles from Thurne Mouth, a triangular piece of water that has been greatly improved in recent years by Commissioners' dredging. On the east side of Horsey Mere is a narrow dyke leading to a large wind pump owned by the National Trust, which visitors can inspect, and on the north of the mere is a narrow canal called Waxham Cut, leading to Bridge Farm. It is possible to moor here and walk to the sea about a mile away. Waxham Cut was originally navigable to Lound Bridge where there used to be a brick works, but this top end is badly silted. This was where the sea broke through in 1947, causing devastation to the fishing in the area for a very long time.

On this route there is an alternative diversion; instead of going up Candle Dyke you can make a lonely, narrow trip to West Somerton. This goes over what remains of Martham Broad.

One of the most interesting places on this trip above Potter is undoubtedly Hickling Broad, looked after by the Norfolk Naturalists' Trust. It is not surprising that Roland Green, the artist, has a studio on the shores of this broad, and many of the birds featured in his paintings can be seen by his studio.

There is a Nature Trail on Hickling Broad run by the Trust which takes twelve people at a time and starts from the Pleasure Boat inn. The trip is an essential introduction to knowing something about the wild life of Broadland, and is particularly interesting for children. Although the Trust looks after the broad, boating is unrestricted, but a permit is required to visit the surrounding reed beds and marshland.

Undoubtedly, the northern rivers are very popular with many holidaymakers. The southern rivers are quite different, but both have their charm and are worthy of equal study. The fact that people tend to congregate more on the northern rivers increases the popularity of the southern ones, which can never be considered overcrowded except at a very few places at peak holiday times.

(*For distances see the map inside end cover*)

CHAPTER THREE

Cruising the Southern Rivers

The visitor to the southern rivers will start from a boatyard or launching point downstream of Norwich, or will have entered these rivers by cruising Breydon Water. (Heed tides, follow instructions, keep to the channel, and Breydon will have no terrors.) On the east of Breydon the River Yare goes to Norwich, and the Waveney goes south to Beccles and Oulton.

River Yare

Going up the Yare, the first mooring is at the Berney Arms. This is the only safe mooring before Reedham, but due allowance must be made for changing tide levels when mooring up. The mill near here is the tallest in Broadland. The first place of consequence is Reedham, 9¾ miles from Gt Yarmouth; when mooring here there is sometimes over 3ft range in tidal levels. There are several boatyards and two inns, the Lord Nelson and the Ship by the river, and others in the village where there are excellent shops. If you are unlucky and have inclement weather, Reedham has an excellent train service and a trip can be made to Norwich or Great Yarmouth.

Above Reedham is the last of the Broadland ferries. The free house, the Ferry Inn, operates the chain ferry for cars and passengers across the Yare. The Archer family, who run the ferry, operate under ancient rights dating back to the Middle Ages. Reedham is also well known for its swing railway bridge, and the artificial new cut running due south to link up with the River Waveney, but more of this later.

Just above the ferry is Hardley Cross, the entrance to the River Chet, leading to Loddon village. At Hardley Cross, Yarmouth officially ends its river control and that of Norwich begins. Loddon has changed greatly since it was put on the Broadland map some years ago. There are new moorings for twenty boats here, managed by the local authority. The White Horse, the King's Head and the Angel are all popular with the visitor, and the church of Holy Trinity is beautiful with numerous treasures. Loddon is nearly 13½ miles from Great Yarmouth, the length of the Chet from the junction to Loddon being 3 miles. Upstream on the main river is Hardley Dyke which leads to the Chequers and a small village, and further upstream is Cantley where there is a large sugar beet factory. Much of the sugar beet for processing was brought by wherry, and it is only in recent years that traffic has ceased. There is still, as can be seen on this river, commercial traffic in the form of coasters going up to Norwich with various cargoes, particularly timber. It is essential on the Yare to remember that these vessels must keep to the deep channel, and sound signals given by their skippers should be promptly obeyed. Near Cantley is the Red Horse Inn. Langley Dyke is shortly reached with the Wherry Inn at the top, and the remains of Langley Abbey near. Above Langley is Fleet Dyke. This is unnavigable and leads to the closed broads of Buckenham and Hassingham. Above the site of the ferry is Short Dyke which leads across Rockland Broad to the staithe. The return journey can be made through the alternative route to Fleet. The broad is shallow and it is essential to keep to the marked channel.

It is now over 17 miles from Great Yarmouth; in two more miles Brundall is reached, although there is a very convenient stop before on the south bank at Coldham Hall Inn, where the landlord has preserved a rarity, a juke box of long ago. This is a penyano, a clockwork-driven barrel organ which plays one of six tunes on insertion of a penny. There is another to be seen in an inn called the Pickerel in a side street in Beccles. At Brundall, with its convenient inns and railway station, there were first class moorings in a long dyke that was dredged by Blakes in 1953 to give a number of moorings off the river in safety, but these have been sold to a private owner.

Opposite Brundall village are the remains of Surlingham Broad, now a series of disconnected pieces of water. It had become very overgrown in recent years, but intensive dredging has now made it possible to explore many parts. This is a place for using the dinghy, and is the area so often written about by Dr E. A. Ellis, whose naturalist writings on the Broads are classics.

Above Surlingham is the Ferry House, but the vehicle ferry no longer operates. Above the ferry are the famous Bramerton Woods, with Bramerton Woods End Inn by the river. Once Whitlingham Marshes have been passed, the outskirts of Norwich are reached, and at Thorpe it is 25½ miles from Great Yarmouth.

At Thorpe there are two routes, the new cut avoiding the railway bridges, or the route which passes the attractive village green and village inns under the railway, but has rarely more than 6ft headroom. The Town House Hotel has particularly fine moorings here and has always been very closely associated with the Broads. At Trowse the Yare turns south and is only navigable to the main road. This junction is used by heavy coasters for turning and great care should be taken. The route eastwards upstream is the River Wensum, under fixed and opening bridges; there is an excellent yacht station near to Thorpe railway station run by the City of Norwich.

It is possible to go above Norwich yacht station, but depths are uncertain, and hire craft should not do so. The head of navigation is in fact New Mills, where fixed sluices prevent any further progress. The jurisdiction of the Yarmouth Port

& Haven Commissioners in fact goes further up the Wensum to Hellesdon, although this section can only be reached by canoe. Moves are being made to create further moorings and a riverside walk in a part of the river at present unused. In times of high water this is a most interesting trip.

The City of Norwich produces a good guide book at a reasonable price. It is difficult to list here all the attractions of a visit, but Shakespearean fans should visit the Maddermarket Theatre, built in the style common to theatres in the time of Elizabeth I. There are also the beautiful cathedral, magnificent parish churches, one of the only two medieval streets left in Britain, Elm Hill, the castle, the city walls and museums; it is truly, as the advertisement says, 'A fine City'. Much of the charm of the Yare stems from the fact that, journeying up the river, one has such a magnificent jewel at the end of the trip. Our American cousins could do worse than have a boat on the Broads, drive to Norwich, pausing for lunch at Thetford, where they could think a little about Tom Paine. More of this later.

In Norwich can be seen strong ties with Europe. The modern town hall would not be out of place in Stockholm. The delightful museum in the Stranger's Hall was a refuge for Flemish weavers. Besides European connections, the name of Worstead lives on in the worsted cloth to be found in every tailor's. This is derived from Worstead village nearly two miles from the canal at Dilham, where the weavers' houses still remain by a magnificent church of cathedral proportions.

River Waveney

The waterways to the south of Breydon can be reached by turning due south at the eastern end to Breydon Water and entering the River Waveney. Here is the first safe mooring between Burgh and Great Yarmouth. The Roman fortress of Burgh Castle is an impressive relic with walls up to 9ft thick. The trip to St Olaves is $9\frac{1}{2}$ miles over the marshes. There is a fixed bridge here with a headroom of 8ft, a good inn, the Bell, and boatyards. Nearby are the remains of an Augustinian Priory. If you moor for a while here, whether you fish or not, you can have an excellent walk to Fritton Decoy, a splendid landlocked broad. Just above St Olaves the artificial cut from Reedham comes in, providing a short cut between the Yare and the Waveney and saving the journey round by Breydon Water. A fixed bridge over the cut has 24ft headroom. This replaced a somewhat Heath Robinson opening bridge which for many years provided some degree of local entertainment. Nearby, Haddiscoe Station is a useful link to places on the Yare and Norwich if land-based pleasures are required in inclement weather.

The Waveney goes on through Somerleyton with the Duke's Head and Brown Inns near. There is a swing bridge here which will be swung open like the one at Reedham unless a red flag is flying to indicate the approach of a train. Oulton Broad is reached 17¾ miles from Great Yarmouth, after passing the junction with the Upper Waveney at Burgh.

Oulton Broad is a Broadland boating centre on a par with Wroxham, with numerous inns, boatyards, shops and chandleries. The development is all located on the west side of the broad. There is a first class yacht station. Navigation for hire craft ceases at Broadland's only lock at Murford. The private owner can lock through into Lake Lothing which connects Oulton Broad with Lowestoft's harbour. This lock will take craft up to 86ft long with a beam of 20ft; the draught available is 9ft. The headroom is unlimited as the bridge is an opening one, but care must be taken in navigating Lowestoft's swing bridge as its height is rather deceptive. There are numerous inns in the locality: the Wherry Hotel has been popular with yachtsmen for many years, although the famous personality, Sid Rich, has moved over to the Cutter Inn at Ely in the Fens. Speedboat racing is a feature of Oulton at certain times of the year.

A useful amenity for children on holiday is Nicholas Everitt Park. This is named after the author, one of whose books

Broadland Sport, written at the turn of the century and well worth seeking in a second-hand bookshop, refers in glowing terms to Oulton, mentioning the Wherry and also the Commodore Inn, The Lady of the Lake and the Waveney. Out of season and often in the evening Broadland perhaps appears not to have changed as much as some people think. The modern visitor at Oulton one evening would recognize the scene depicted by Everitt seventy-five years ago:

> 'It is evening. The sun is sinking behind the Fishrow Hills, causing the dark tops of the Scotch fir trees, which peep over their brow, to give the appearance of a ridge of rocks. The broad lies calm and tranquil, except where a few swans disturb its bosom, or idlers in boats are drifting in a listless manner to and fro. The yachts have laid to and made up for the night. The wherries are unable to proceed, except with the assistance of the unwieldy quant, and the wind has died away to a whisper, which is usual in broadland at sunset. From one end of the broad comes the lowing of cows faintly echoed from the marshes beyond Whitecast; from the other the noise of children playing in the street, or bathing in the sheltered bays. We as visitors are enchanted beyond measure—how can we fail to be otherwise?'

Lowestoft, for the private owner who can take his boat down from Oulton, is well worth a visit. This fishing port has got great character, and with luck you might find some real oak-smoked kippers. It is said that these kippers can be spotted by their lightish buff colour.

Retracing one's steps to explore the upper Waveney, there is the delightful village of Burgh St Peter; its fifteenth century church has a thatched roof. The mooring by the stores at the Waveney Hotel is excellent. The river to Beccles is pleasant, running through flat meadows, but there are very few moorings and the villages are a good distance from the river. This area is one that has been put forward for development by the creation of artificial broads. Approaching Beccles, the flat landscape is broken by Boathouse Hill. There are good moorings here and a walk to the top gives a remarkably good view of the river. Beccles is an attractive country town with well-equipped yacht station, of which the only handicap for the yachting visitor is Beccles Bridge. The restricted headroom here at times of high water has been known to keep a number of craft upstream of the bridge for several days, but this is a rare occurrence. The church of St Michael has a detached bell tower. It is worth going to the top of the church and looking at the view, particularly fine towards Geldeston. As a boating centre there are many yachting shops as well as the usual ones, and the town is well endowed with inns, of which the King's Head in the town centre is well known.

It is worth while seeking out the Pickerel Inn, where there is an automatic barrel organ. Some years ago the BBC did a feature on the Waveney, in which the Pickerel Inn and landlord played their part. The river is navigable for only a short distance to Geldeston above Beccles—reference will be made to the closed navigation later on. In the spring of 1958, Jimmy Hoseason, whose bluebirds are splashed all over Broadland, was weaned away from the affairs of the hire cruiser business to join the author in a trip from Beccles to Bungay in a light craft with an outboard motor which could be portaged round the old locks. We took a message from the Mayor of Beccles to the Town Reeve of Bungay. The latter is an unusual office dating back to Saxon times, and this, like many other things, makes Bungay an interesting town. The trip between the locks in the evening over completely deserted waters enabled one to see what Broadland looked like many years ago, as there was no development on the river above the locks. It is only 3 miles from Beccles to Geldeston, which makes Geldeston 17¾ miles from Oulton. At Geldeston there are two arms, one the dyke leading to the village where there is an inn called the Wherry, the other leading to the Locks, the old Lock House for Shipmeadow (or Geldeston) Lock, also an inn. In spite of the profusion of wherry traffic, it is surprising that so few inns were called the Wherry. There was one at Paston on the North Walsham Canal until recent years, and another near the River Blyth at Halesworth. This Wherry Inn is particularly attractive to a number of local people as it serves a brew of local ale which comes from Southwold. The Locks is a very remote inn. It is difficult to get to it by road, and local cattle using the road have also had navigation difficulties and landed in the dyke. Miss Ellis on occasions gives visitors very explicit instructions as to how to retrieve cows from dykes. The inn is primitive, lit by candles, a relic of a bygone age. The system whereby patrons are handed a bill at the end of the evening is quite unique. Susan, as Miss Ellis is affectionately called, relates to two geese, one called Susan and the other Grumpy—but let the visitor find out the rest of the story for himself. Geldeston is the end of the journey.

The southern rivers are less obvious in their charms than the northern ones; they are less crowded, but when one reflects that the great East Anglian naturalist, Dr E. A. Ellis, presides over the Nature Reserve at Surlingham, one realises that the southern rivers certainly have something.

(*For distances, see the map inside end cover*)

CHAPTER FOUR

Broads Hire Cruising

The hire cruise organisation on the Broads is the most highly sophisticated boat holiday organisation to be found anywhere. It is difficult to pinpoint the exact date when boat hiring came to Broadland. The author's father remembers being taken aboard a hired yacht that had been let out by Smoker Southgate before 1900. Payne-Jennings in his travels around the Broads taking photograph for his famous illustrated books on the Broads was hiring boats from 1874 onwards. It was probably the old wherrymen who discovered through taking out organised parties like school treats during the summer that there was money to be made out of boat hire. The Londoner went to the Broads on the Great Eastern Railway, and the Midland & Great Northern Railway brought in visitors from the Midlands. These visitors undoubtedly holidayed on the coast, and after having taken drives around the Broads in 'brakes', the old horse-drawn chars-à-banc, soon created a demand to go afloat. It was evident that the locals on the Broads were then catering for the visitor, for as long ago as 1881, the Malsters at Ranworth sold London beer and the local brew side by side.

The first agent to book was Mr Brown at St Olaves, who issued a brochure as early as 1890. After 1900 development

Page 51 (*above*) The Rising Sun, Coltishall, one of the most popular moorings on the Bure near the head of the navigation; (*below*) River Waveney at Beccles during the TV series *Riverbeat*. Broadland is often a good subject for TV with its holiday opportunities.

Page 52 (*above*) Railway swing bridge opened for shipping on the River Yare at Reedham; (*below*) Thorpe village near Norwich, River Yare.

really started, Mr Harry Blake being the great pioneer in the hire craft business. The Blake organisation was founded in 1902, and has the largest fleet of Broads boats.

The late Paul C. Dewhurst, a great authority on the Broads, who took many invaluable photographs, used to scour the Broadland boat yards in an old belt driven motor cycle for a suitable yacht to hire. His technique might not make the author popular with some boat yards, but inspecting the yard and the boat before you hire it is recommended. In spite of brochures and salesmanship, you will learn much more by looking at the boat first if it is accessible.

Harry Blake who started it all, noted his bookings in 1907 in a pocket diary, a free gift from a building society, and the next year he represented most of the boatowners on the Broads. He took a three-line announcement in *The Daily Mail* which cost 4s 6d (22½p) and brought in 400 replies. The 1908 catalogue listed 43 cabin sailing yachts, the season being from mid-July to the end of August. The season now is almost six months.

Blakes office in London was at 10 Basinghall Street, London, EC2; in 1916 it went to Newgate Street, near St Paul's, thence to Fleet Street in 1945, but left the City in 1952 for Albemarle Street. The main office of Blakes is at Hoveton St John, Norfolk, although the north bank is commonly thought to be Wroxham as well. Blakes office in London will continue to be open from January to March, the peak booking season, to assist personal callers at Albemarle Street.

The Blakes organisation at the present moment has some thirty-nine yards, distinguished by a red and white flag with the name Blakes and a large A printed in blue on it. All boats carry a plate with a similar motif. The organisation books cruisers with from two to ten berths, also yachts and auxiliary yachts. In addition, houseboats are hired out, usually with a rowing boat and occasionally with a day launch. Day launches and light craft can also be hired, and holiday accommodation on short by the Broads and on the Norfolk coast. Houseboats

Holiday Cruising on the Broads and Fens

THE WHERRY-YACHTS

"Bertha," "Elsie," "Kate," "Diligent," & "Lucy,"

BELONGING TO

Messrs. PRESS BROTHERS,

NORTH WALSHAM,

Are fitted with every Convenience for the Enjoyment of Parties wishing to Visit

The Rivers and Broads of Norfolk.

They contain: Ladies' Cabin, 7 ft. long, 9 ft. wide, and 6 ft. high, to sleep 3 or 4 Ladies, and are fitted with Washstand, Looking-Glass, Lockers, &c., &c.

Gentlemen's Cabin, 14 ft. long, 9 ft. wide, and 6 ft. high, to sleep 4 or 6 Gentlemen; this Cabin is used in the day time for a Dining Saloon, and is fitted with a table down the centre, and sitting space for 8 or 10.

The Cabins throughout are furnished with Blinds, soft Cushions, plenty of Rugs, and are lighted at night by lamps; they are divided by a gangway leading from the Deck, and a W. C. entered from either the fore or aft Cabin, and private to each.

Two men are provided by the owners to look after and Sail the Yachts, and are under the direction of the Party hiring the Boat; they will attend to the cooking, cleaning, and washing up, and to the wants of the Party on board.

When sailing, a seat is provided on the fore deck of the Yacht, and a 'Jolly Boat' accompanies each.

The Yachts are provided with all necessary Glass, Crockery, Table Linen, Knives, Forks, Spoons, &c., &c., and the men's Cabin is fitted with a good Cooking Stove.

When required a Piano can be provided at an extra cost of 15 shillings per week.

The Yachts are so arranged as to be able to visit all the Norfolk and Suffolk Broads:—Barton, Wroxham, Hickling, South Walsham, Horsey Mere, Mutford, Oulton, and all places of interest on the Rivers.

Parties are required to go on board wherever the owners may desire, but can leave the Yachts at any place convenient to themselves by giving a week's notice.

For Terms and further particulars, apply—

PRESS BROTHERS,

North Walsham, Norfolk.

Wherry-yachts: an advertisement of 1887

are a popular start for young families. They are usually moored near to a boat yard and have main services.

Inquiries should be addressed to Blakes (Norfolk Broads Holidays) Ltd, Wroxham, Norwich, NOR 4IZ: telephone Wroxham 2141.

The rowing boat is a useful start for waterway exploration, and a family will naturally graduate to a cruiser or yacht when they get older, although the houseboat also has its uses for writers, painters and fishermen.

All the agencies hire out yachts. Although declining in numbers it is perhaps as well to remember that the only other place on the inland waterways of Britain you can hire a yacht is Lake Windermere.

The great development in the hiring industry, which made the industry what it is today, was the period between the wars. Harry Blake and Jack Robinson were the booking agents, and they helped to form trade associations, boat standards and a code of practice for running a responsible business. The names of the men who built up this industry are Ernest Collins, Jack Powles, Herbert Hipperson, Alfred Ward, Herbert Woods, Clifford Hill, Ted Landamore, and many others who will always be remembered, although there are many changes even in Broadland. The family boat yard is in some cases being taken over by companies.

There are other agencies, one of which carries the name of Hoseason, whose yards are designated by a blue bird, the motif appearing on the flag at the boat yards and on the boats. Like Blakes, they act as letting agents for a network of some sixty boat yards. Whilst Blakes organisation is owned by its boat yard members, Hoseason is more of a letting agent. Both endeavour to enforce a number of basic standards and offer a similar range of boats.

Recently in an interview Jimmy Hoseason said to the author:

> Our visitors no longer go boating in the old sense of the word. Today's boating enthusiast expects comforts and

modern facilities aboard his boat. There are only a few of the old Spartan-type boats left. All the boats in our fleet now have hot water and a refrigerator; the family size boats have shower baths; and more and more boats are being fitted with space heating. Television is available as an optional extra on all boats.

His organisation offers modern Bermuda and sloop-rigged yachts at Martham; houseboats, some moored individually in private moorings, others available in holiday centres; day-use self-drive cabin motor launches are available for hire with these houseboats and Hoseasons' riverside bungalows.

Hoseasons' operations began in 1945, and the business is now the largest self-catering holiday company in the country. It also offers many holiday bungalows and chalets in East Anglia which are ideal starting points for exploring the rivers and broads by launch. Hoseasons also act as booking agents for a number of well known companies on the River Thames and canals.

Inquiries should be addressed to Hoseasons Sunshine Holidays, Sunway House, Oulton Broad, Suffolk—telephone Lowestoft 62181.

There are two other agencies, the Bradbeer Red Whale Fleet based at Lowestoft, and Broads Holidays Limited of Great Yarmouth.

R. H. Bradbeer Limited, for many years based at 7 Battery Green Road, Lowestoft, is administered by Mr Eric Mathew. The Bradbeer Company has about 250 boats and Broads Holidays Ltd, over 100. The latter organisation is associated with the marina at Caister Road, Yarmouth. There has always been co-operation on vital Broads matters between Mr Mathew, Mr Hoseason and Mr Brooker when he was at Blakes. It is interesting to note that these four commercial organisations who had nothing to gain, did in fact strongly support Broadland becoming a National Park, though other sectional interests showed little enthusiasm.

In addition to the agencies, there are a number of firms who let craft privately direct to customers. It is impossible to list these, but *Motor Boat & Yachting, published* bi-weekly, carries useful advertisements not only for the agencies but also for individual hire firms. Some mention ought to be made of one of these concerns, R. Moore & Sons (Wroxham) Ltd. This is a family business personally supervised by the directors, and one of the family will usually see you on your way.

Is it best to book through an agency or an individual firm? It usually comes down to the simple fact that you get what you pay for. Further, in some cases checks are made that boats are not let two years running to a bad, neglectful hirer.

Talking of costs, and with rising prices these have to be watched very carefully, it is perhaps as well to look at what it can cost and what you get for your money. You can hire a self-drive motor cruiser on the East Anglian waterways that offers you every comfort for everybody: soft beds, comfortable seating in a spacious saloon, a modern kitchen with every labour-saving convenience: hot and cold running water, a refrigerator and a full size domestic cooker, a sun deck, a shower bath, and a powerful engine that has simple controls that can be mastered in but a few minutes, even if you have never driven a car. The cost of hiring these boats is modest. Sample of total weekly holiday costs for a party of six adults on a boating holiday in 1971:

Boat hire	Luxury diesel-powered cruiser to sleep six adults at 1972 peak rates	£101.00
Fuel	20 gallons of diesel oil at marine rates	3.50
A map	Map of the waterways	.20
Fishing licences	Two fishing licences at 50p ...	1.00
Housekeeping, etc	Say £2.00 a day	14.00
Dining out	Make it two nights for six, including wine at £1.25	15.00

Refreshments	Say £1.00 per head	6.00
Entertainment	A visit to a theatre and an amusement park	4.00
Garaging	An under-cover garage for the car	1.00
		£145.70

That is £24 a head, or £4 each per day, all-in. In off-peak periods it works out even lower—down to £15 each per week. Compare these prices with a holiday abroad. Official Board of Trade figures show the average cost of an economical week's holiday abroad is £62. Why, even a week in an English hotel will cost you at least £30 for full board, and that does not include beer money or entertainment.

Yards vary in the facilities they offer, and the number of flags in the catalogue does not always indicate above or below average boatyards, but generally there are facilities for water and fuel and mooring during the week for craft belonging to the group.

Soon boat yards will also have to provide facilities for emptying the toilets which under recent river authority bye-laws will not be permitted to be discharged straight into the water. In any case, please always use the short toilets wherever possible.

If in the slightest doubt about any matter, always refer to your nearest Association boat yard or the office of the company owning the boat. Above all, boats tend to be almost human, and things go wrong in the best of organised families, so if you have any doubts or worries do let the people know what has happened. You will be surprised how interested those who run the boats are in their business. The truth is you can make more money in other enterprises than you can out of a boat hire business, but the successful boat hirer has to care about the business and like it. and it may be no surprise to the reader to learn that when almost the last of the holidaymakers have gone, the leaves are disappearing from the trees, and Broadland is becoming a reminder of what it was like one hundred years ago, you will find several parties of boat hirers enjoying their own beloved Broadsland as much as any holidaymaker who had seen it for the first time. When you have cruised the Broads for many years you may be lucky enough to enjoy the company of that coterie of old diehards who sail rivers as avidly as the wherrymen of bygone days.

As a tailpiece, how about those elderly folk who would like a taste of Broadland cruising, or the organised party who would like a day out in Broadland all together with an experienced skipper? They are excellently catered for by the Broads Tours Ltd organisation of Wroxham. There is the *Princess Margaret,* which is called the children's boat, the *Princess Mary,* the *Princess Elizabeth,* the *Marchioness,* and the widest boat of all, the *Marina.* The little booklet you can buy here for 12½p written by Mr C. A. Hannaford, is good value for money. So well known is this organisation that when a letter was addressed to the Captain of the Boats, Wroxham, Norfolk, it was delivered where it belonged, to Broads Tours. Perhaps it is understandable, for the last time the boats were counted there were eighteen of them.

CHAPTER FIVE

Closed Broads and Navigations

(See also the list of nature sites and reserves in ch. 1, p 18)

A number of broads which in the past were open to navigation are now closed (see list on p. 67). On the Bure, Hudson's Bay, Hoveton Great Broad, Decoy Broad, Cockshoot Broad and Ranworth Broad are all closed. *The New Oarsman's Guide* published in 1896 shows Hoveton Great Broad as being closed, as well as the Little Broad, although Emerson sailed in his wherry *The Maid of the Mist* through the broad early in 1891. Other broads, for example, Strumpshaw, Sutton and Martham, are now reduced to navigation channels.

Various causes account for the closing. Some landowners have claimed that the fishing and shooting on certain broads was exclusively their own, and have closed the water to the public entirely. There was little incentive in past days to stop them. The holiday yachtsman came to the Broads formerly only for six weeks in the year. The sailing wherries were decreasing as trade moved off the water. As for other Broadsmen, they were often the employees of the landowners and equally keen to keep the water private. Even so, there has been opposition to the disappearance of public waters.

The enthusiast making researches in this connection should take care. It is often claimed that Dilham Broad has disappeared. Certainly the wherries traded across a sheet of water bearing this name just above Honing Lock, but in truth Dilham Broad was the mill pond of the mill and was entirely man made, and after the mill ceased functioning the broad reverted to sedge and reed. In spite of the loss of cruising area by closure of broads, the number remaining open have received such treatment from the Commissioners with their dredging programme that the position is probably beter now than it was before the First War. The decline of the sailing yacht for hire on the Broads, although happily not by the private owner, is in some measure due to the congestion that can occur at holiday weekends at certain places.

The closed broads provide a haven for the naturalist, and the Norfolk Naturalist Trust now owns or leases seven areas in Broadland. (See ch. 1 p. 18.) These include Hickling, Barton, Surlingham, Alderfen Broad, Ranworth Broad, which with Cockshoot Broad, forms part of the Bure Marshes Nature Reserve. This Reserve gathers in all 1,019 acres, of which 200 are woodland. It is an unrivalled series of aquatic, fen and marsh communities which are typical of this part of the Broads. Not only do they form a valuable refuge for bird life, but they show the sequence of events which vegetation follows in the absence of any disturbance by man. It was in this area that researches were made which showed that the Broads were in many cases man made in the Middle Ages for peat digging. A permit is required to visit this area, and application should be made by intending visitors to the Nature Conservancy, East Anglia Region, Norwich.

Fritton Decoy, as its name suggests, is a place where duck-decoying is still carried out. Fritton is a beautiful lake surrounded by trees and approximately three miles long. Rowing boats can be hired. Ormesby, Rollesby and Filby Broads are landlocked, with delightful woodland surrounding Ormesby and Rollesby. The small Lily Broad leads out of Rollesby. All these are a haven for the angler, with rowing boats available for hire. There is an unnavigable connection with the River

Bure, called Muck Fleet, which passes a tiny broad called Little Broad, on the way to the main river. The drainage authority for this area has the enchanting name of Muck Fleet & South Flegg Internal Drainage Broad. Crome's Broad is part of the How Hill estate owned by the Norfolk County Council. As yet there is no access to it, but it has only recently been taken into public ownership. There used to be a staithe on this broad. Buckenham and Hassingham Broads have no public access through Fleet Dyke. Blackhorse Broad is open in the summer only, a compromise arrangement that was made by the late Herbert Woods with the owners when Blakes were conducting a battle to reopen closed broads.

Good inns are The Fox & Hounds at Filby and The Eel's Foot on Ormesby Broad, The Sportsman's Arms at the top of Rollesby, all useful places for refreshment. The Eel's Foot was a popular fishermen's inn when Payne-Jennings toured the Broads from 1885 onwards carrying photographic equipment weighing hundreds of pounds, which produced photographs which have stood the test of time.

Broadland has more than its fair share of closed navigations. Enthusiasts are always disturbed at the continued closure of these old waterways. In truth, the position is not as bad as it might appear. The splendid work of the Commissioners since the war has had a saving effect. The River Chet at Loddon which, for many years, was difficult to use except at high water, has been dredged and transformed. Waxham Cut an artificial waterway leading northwards from Horsey Mere, was saved from closure, dredged and kept open to Bridge Farm where only a short walk brings you to the sea, but the remainder of the Cut to Lound Bridge near Palling is weeded up and impassable. It is doubtful if opening this narrow waterway at the top end would serve any useful purpose.

The three main closed navigations are the Bure above Coltishall to Aylsham, the River Waveney from Geldeston, Shipmeadow Lock to Bungay, and the North Walsham Canal to Antingham Pond. The latter waterway is in fact the Ant River

Navigation. The water connection to Dilham is often referred to as a branch of the canal, but this was never the case. The dyke to the Dilham brickworks was a private canal constructed to join up with the Smallburgh River. Although derelict until 1965, this route has been dredged and is now open.

The navigation rights on the River Bure above Coltishall were abandoned by the Minister of Transport in 1927. The locks had in fact been out of order since 1912 when they were damaged by floods. The navigation rights on the River Waveney above Geldeston were abandoned in 1934. The North Walsham Canal was the subject of a proposed closure order, which was never carried out.

The rivers Bure and Waveney are used by canoes and other manually propelled craft. Those who do make an excursion on these deserted waters should take great care not to interfere with angling. There have been suggestions on a number of occasions that the two rivers should be reopened, but there is no means of reviving the extinguished rights, and often road or other construction has taken place.

On the River Bure Navigation the first lock has been converted into a fixed sluice, but above the Bure is wide, a little weedy and a sluggish stream. There is a three mile stretch to the site of Buxton Mill, now unhappily demolished. The lock has completely disappeared and is underneath the road. The section from Lamas Church through Oxnead Lock towards Burgh is very fine. Oxnead Lock is still in existence with a fixed dam at the top of the lock, but the bottom gates have long disappeared. Burgh Lock, just three miles from Aylsham, is a real teaser for the canal enthusiast to find, and consists of little more than two heaps of rubble in a small spinney of young trees. The fifth lock is only one mile from Aylsham, but at the head of navigation the old wharves can still be seen, together with some of the warehouses.

Aylsham is a pleasant country town, but Aylsham Parish Church is the only medieval building there. Aylsham linen was highly prized and sought after by royalty in the time of

Edward III. Blickling Hall is two miles from Aylsham, set in glorious wooded countryside. You need a full afternoon to see this enormous building, although from the great façade you get no idea of the size of the place. No less than three generations of Boleyns resided here, but of all the famous people associated with Blickling, Ann Boleyn, of course, is the best known. This National Trust property is open from May to September from 2 pm to 5.30 pm, Wednesdays, Thursdays, Sundays and Bank Holidays.

A canoe trip to Aylsham gives a fair idea of what cruising on the Broads must have been like before the turn of the century, although, of course, the wherry is absent. Here as everywhere else in Broadland in days gone by it was hardly possible to take a photograph without including a wherry in it.

The great floods of 1912 did damage to all three navigations, but the Bure never recovered and was more seriously damaged than the others. A boat slide has been provided at Coltishall by The Broads Society to allow light craft to use the upper reaches of the river. Aylsham to Coltishall is nine and a quarter miles.

The Waveney has excited more attention than the Bure from navigation revivalists. It is certainly a very pretty river above Geldeston. The river is affected by tides up to Ellingham. Here the lock was partly filled in when the large new sluice gates were constructed. Ellingham has a delightfully white boarded water mill, a popular subject for photographers and painters, although unfortunately like so many buildings of this type it no longer acts as a mill but is a private residence.

The river is wide and clear to the next lock at Wainford, although this lock is sometimes called Ditchingham. By the lock are large maltings. The section of river from Geldeston is very fine sailing water for dinghies. There is more shallow water above Wainford, although generally the depth is at least three feet to the staithe at Bungay. The distance from Bungay to Geldeston is four and a quarter miles. Geldeston Lock is also called Shipmeadow Lock.

The canal to North Walsham was authorised by an Act of 1812, and was completed with six locks to Antingham Bone Mills in 1826. In 1912 there was disastrous flooding in East Norfolk, caused by 7in of rainfall in twenty-four hours; the canal bank at Bacton Wood was broken and part of the road washed into the canal below Ebridge Bridge. The section from Swafield Bridge to Antingham Pond was closed in 1927. The waterway was used by wherries until 1935 through the bottom three locks, although the top two locks at Swafield went out of use in 1890 and Bacton Wood Lock ceased to be usable in 1912.

The present position is that the top two Swafield Locks have disappeared completely; Bacton Wood Lock, Ebridge and Briggate, together with Honing are in a bad state, although in all cases apart from the lock at Honing, the top gates hold up water.

The waterway as a whole goes through very attractive countryside, but is in a derelict condition, though short branches could give moorings or a marina.

The wherries which used this canal until 1935 had timber hulls about 53ft long, plus 6ft of rudder. They were adapted for sailing and easy lowering of sail and mast, and their extreme beam was 12½ft. Their mast with counterbalance sail and gear weighed some 2½ tons. They were heavily timbered, especially at the tabernacle as there were no side shrouds, but only a single forestay. Their freight on the canal was 20 tons, and they had a 'sliding keel' about 9in deep for holding to windward in deep water. This keel was detachable and could be detached in about twenty minutes. Navigation ceased on the waterway in 1935, but apart from the section from the ruins of Honing Lock to Briggate which is shallow, it is a very attractive proposition for light craft as the top gates of two locks still hold up water. Certainly this section of Broadland is the loneliest of all.

North Walsham was mainly destroyed by fire in 1600, but is a delightful town, with a good deal of character, which was largely given to it in Tudor times when it was famous for wool weaving. There is a magnificent church with cathedral-like qualities and with the remains of a tower 150ft high. There are several crosses to be seen in the countryside near North Walsham, one to the Peasants' Revolt of 1381. It was on 17 June 1381 that the labourers met on Mousehold Heath.

There is a very fine mill at Briggate and also Ebridge, although in neither case do they use water power from the river. The canal carries many more water lilies than occasional canoeists, but it is surely a navigation which should be reopened for the pleasure of all. It is essential that craft continue to use the canal, otherwise the navigation can be abandoned on the grounds that it is never used. Application to use the waterway should be made to the North Walsham Canal Company Ltd, Ebridge Mills, North Walsham.

Closed Broads and Navigations

Broads and lakes not open for navigation
(From *A Regional Strategy for Water Recreation 1971*)

Norfolk

Alderfen Broad (13 acres—landlocked—originally 27 acres)
Belaugh Broad (3 acres—private and too shallow—originally 12 acres)
Blackfleet Broad (5 acres—private and too shallow—originally 12 acres)
Buckenham and Hassingham Broad (6 acres—originally 26 acres)
Burntfen Broad (15 acres—landlocked)
Calthorpe Broad (3 acres—landlocked—originally 16 acres)
Crome's Broad (12 acres—originally 15 acres)
Cockshoot Broad (8 acres—private—originally 29 acres)
Decoy Broad (18 acres—private—originally 29 acres)
Filby Broad (83 acres—used for sailing—originally 116 acres)
Hoveton Great Broad (47 acres—private—originally 103 acres)
Hudson's Bay (3 acres—private and too shallow—originally 15 acres)
Ormesby Broad North (139 acres—originally 189 acres)
Ormesby Broad South (88 acres—originally 121 acres)
Ranworth Broad (59 acres—private—originally 141 acres)
Rollesby & Lily Broads (61 acres—originally 97 acres)
Strumpshaw Broad (2 acres—private and too shallow—originally 22 acres)
Upton Broad (4 acres—landlocked—originally 29 acres)

E. Suffolk

Barnby Broad (7 acres—landlocked—originally 27 acres)
Flixton Decoy (15 acres—landlocked—originally 18 acres)
Fritton Lake (150 acres—originally 163 acres)

CHAPTER SIX

The Fens, Introduction and Background

Fenland is a very wide expression, but is generally considered to be that area of 2,500 square miles which extends from south of Lincoln to Suffolk, and from St Ives to King's Lynn. This area is, in the main, a shallow basin consisting on the eastern side of clay and silt beds, laid down in brackish water in ancient times when the sea came much further inland. On the western side peat was formed, in land waterlogged by discharges from many rivers and streams, and was therefore under fresh water conditions. The area is a very ancient one, and for a proper study of the formation of the region, particularly in reference to the peat, one must go back as far, at least, as the last ice age. Numerous forests once covered part of the area, but in time the trees were killed and sank into the peat which, over the years, covered almost the whole area. These bog oaks constituted a very real problem to many a Fenland farmer reclaiming the fen for agriculture as they were immensely hard, having been preserved in the peat for thousands of years. A specimen of bog oak can be seen in the bar of the Ferry Boat Inn at Holywell.

Certain fringe areas have been inhabited since Roman times, but after 400 AD it seems likely that the Fen country was for all practical purposes uninhabited. The Romans carried out some drainage work in the area, and built the Caer Dyke, which traversed the western side of the Fens. Traces of this can still be found on the route which it is assumed to follow from Cambridge to Lincoln. As the Saxons took over, Fenland became a kind of no-man's land between the two kingdoms of East Anglia and Mercia. As Christianity came to these islands, some of the monks took to the Fens to establish their religious institutions, for example, Ely and Crowland. Such a region of reed and swamp formed a natural defence against marauders of various kinds who came to these shores, particularly against the ferocious Danes. This is the country of Hereward the Wake, the Lord of Bourne. After the Norman Conquest, the chieftains in the northern Fens resisted the Normans, although eventually bargains were made, but Hereward would have none of these. The story about his valiant defence of the Isle of Ely can be found in *Camp of Refuge* by Charles MacFarlane. William the Conqueror's attack on the Isle took place in 1071, and J. Wentworth Day in *The History of the Fens* calls it '. . . the last and toughest resistance he had to meet in England. The defence of the Isle remains an undying epic of imperishable valour'. When you visit the Ferry Boat at Holywell to see the bog oak you can reflect that this great Englishman also passed this way over the ferry.

Fenland has changed out of all recognition since the Conquest. Now drained and worked, it contains some of the richest farming land in Britain. Often represented as flat, uninteresting country, there are, nevertheless, areas of great beauty, as, for example, between St Ives and Huntingdon. The Rivers Welland, Witham, Glen, Nene, Great Ouse, Little Ouse and Cam have been subdued by vast drainage works, but scattered over the area can be found old beds of rivers which have been diverted into new channels. One can cruise over most of the area, but it must be remembered that practically all waterways here are primarily drainage channels.

In the past the rivers were much used for transport, for roads were bad and scarce in the Middle Ages. In 1617 letters patent were issued to John Gason to improve navigation on the Great Ouse. Gason's patent laid down that he had to pay an annual rent of 40s (£2) to the Crown, although he was able to receive all profits from the rivers which he made into navigations. He assigned his rights seven months later to Arnold Spencer, one of the pioneers of seventeenth century river navigation. These rights were assigned jointly to Thomas Girton who constructed sluices on the river. The navigation eventually went as far inland as Bedford.

Trading continued on the river for many years, then fell away, but the history of the many lawsuits connected with the navigation are a complete story in themselves. Several attempts were made to revive the navigation to Bedford, and when the Great Ouse Catchment Board was formed in 1930, the locks were restored upstream as far as Eaton Socon. The head of navigation has been Tempsford Bridge on the Great North Road for many years.

The Great Ouse River Authority, successor of the River Board which followed the Catchment Board, were until recently not a navigation authority, though they have now taken powers to become one. Meanwhile the Great Ouse Restoration Society, a body registered as a charity, was formed in 1951, and since that date has raised funds for navigation works on the locks from Bedford downstream. Sympathetic design of the drainage installations enabled navigation doors to be fitted. Bedford Town lock and Cardington lock have been restored, and a lock at Roxton is being built to replace the old structure. Before very long we hope that the navigation will be restored through to Bedford.

The Nene, like the Welland (see Chapter 10) has also been the subject of much drainage work. Both are old navigations, the Welland dating from the seventeenth, the Nene from the eighteenth, century. After 1900 the Nene declined as a navigation, and de Salis in his *Bradshaw* (1918 edition) recorded the works as being in indifferent condition. There were no less than ten navigation weirs which were a very old type and a great hindrance to boats, and the river between Peterborough and Wisbech was seriously obstructed by shoals. The rebuilding of the locks and the construction of the large electrically-operated lock by the inn with the curious name of Dog-in-a-Doublet, has now made the Nene one of the best maintained navigations in the country. The navigation body is the Welland & Nene River Authority.

The expressions North Level, Middle Level and South Level are frequently encountered in this area. The North Level is roughly the area between the Welland and the Nene. The Middle Level, better known to intrepid inland waterway travellers, is the area between the Nene and the Ouse, where the waterways conect the River Nene near Peterborough and the Ouse. South Level is the area south of the Ouse, and the term South Level rivers is sometimes used for the Great Ouse and its tributaries.

Before dealing with these cruising waters in detail, it is well to grasp that the Fenland navigational network is based on rivers and drainage channels which, at certain times of the year and under certain conditions, carry tremendous discharges of water. This important seasonal drainage, coupled with the regular draining of the whole area which is causing the Fens to sink, causes additional subsidence, while the rivers rise higher and higher above the surrounding countryside. Some idea of the land shrinkage can be gained from the Holme Post. In 1851 an iron column was sunk into solid clay near Holme Fen. By 1860 it was 4ft 9in out of the ground, and by 1932 it was 10ft 8in out. It is now some 12ft above the surface of the ground and there is still 10ft of peat remaining below. (See Major Gordon Fowler in the *Geographical Journal,* 1933 LXXXL 149.) The shrinkage of soil is not constant but varies all over the Fen country, so adding to the difficulties of the drainage authorities.

Fenland folk of course who earned their livelihood by fishing, wild-fowling, etc, hated the drainage experts who sought to turn their Fenland into agricultural land. In 1490 Bishop

Morton of Ely cut a new course of the River Nene from Peterborough, by-passing the old course of the river which now forms the Middle Level Drainage Navigations in March and district. In the mid-seventeenth century Sir Cornelius Vermuyden carried out the most extensive of all the early drainage works. The full story of this is in L. E. Harris's book *Vermuyden and the Fens.* Mr Harris gives the credit, long overdue, to this great drainage pioneer who had been subject to many misconceptions. There were vast lakes known as meres at Whittlesey and Ramsey, and also Trundle Mere and Ugg Mere. Whittlesey was the largest, covering over 1,600 acres, and when this was drained in the nineteenth century, the value of the land increased tenfold. The New Bedford River, 100ft broad and 21 miles long, stands as the largest drainage work carried out by the early pioneers. However, the sluices constructed at Denver collapsed in 1713. The present structure, built by the Swiss engineer Labelye in the mid-eighteenth century, still stands in its lonely majesty at a blustery corner of the Fens. Mother Nature is not so easily tamed, and there have been several disastrous floods since those early drainage works were constructed, but none so bad as the flood of 1947, which followed the bad winter of 1946-7. Damage has been estimated at £20 million. Great gaps were torn in the river walls, the worst one being at Earith. In the neighbourhood of Ely 15,000 acres were under water. Although the floods commenced in March, 6,000 acres of Haddenham Fen were still under water in June.

The problem was then tackled on a sufficiently large scale, in the Great Ouse Flood Protection Scheme. This million pound operation, carried out by the Great Ouse River Authority, now protects half a million acres of land. Commenced under the direction of W. E. Doran, engineer to the Authority, the works were completed by his successor W. K. Masters. It is a pity that Vermuyden could not have been invited to the opening ceremony, for many of his ideas were incorporated in the work. W. K. Masters has contributed a number of accounts of the scheme to help those who travel the area to understand some of the problems. On the map you will find the new channels described as Relief Channel and Cut-off Channel. Masters says:

> 'The Cut-off Channel discharges freely into the Relief Channel without any control sluice. The Cut-off Channel passes beneath the Rivers Wissey and Little Ouse by means of inverted syphons, and boat users travelling up the River Wissey will pass over the top of the Cut-off Channel a short distance downstream of Stoke Ferry and will then notice a sluice gate which, in normal times, is always left fully open. In flood times this gate will be closed and another gate a short distance away will be opened enabling the flood discharge in the River Wissey to pass down a diversion channel into the Cut-off Channel and so into the Relief Channel and out to sea.'

Certain of these sections are suitable for sailing and there is also a section set aside for water skiing. The huge reservoir at Diddington called Grafham Water has helped to keep a flow of water in the Great Ouse during dry spells. This reservoir provides an abundance of sailing.

Other waterways remain, which cannot be called navigations, but yet can be explored with dinghy or canoe, or for pleasant walking. The closed navigation to Bedford is being slowly reopened, but the navigation to Thetford, although a statutory one originally vested in Thetford Corporation, has long been closed. It only had single-gate flash-locks, and new locks would have to be built to carry navigation to Thetford, an expensive undertaking but worth considering long-term, as Thetford is expanding as an overspill town.

The Lark was previously navigable to Bury St Edmunds, but the flow of water in the river is such that it could carry little traffic if restored. Before the last war the Great Ouse Catchment Board rebuilt two locks. One, at Icklingham, is in perfect working order, although isolated from the rest of the river. Effectively, the river could be reopened to Mildenhall and Barton Mills. Beyond here it has been put through a syphon, but the bold navigator with a dinghy and an outboard can go a long way up the Lark.

The other closed navigation which is almost completely forgotten is the Thorney River. This used to leave the Nene and run northwards to Thorney Village. It is a pretty little backwater, which still holds water, but the lock has gone and there is a fixed sluice in its place, which is a pity. A number of other lodes, like Soham and Cottenham, were used for small boats many years ago, but were never navigations in the accepted sense of the word. There was also a lock down by the railway dock at Ely.

The saddest closure of all was the Wisbech Canal linking Outwell to Wisbech. This gave a short cut through to the Middle Level from the Nene to the Ouse. It was abandoned as long ago as 1924 and has been a bone of contention with the local authorities ever since.

Fenland is a different world from Broadland, although it has the same air and glorious skies. The Ouse has seen considerable development for the private boatowner, but there are comparatively few hire craft on the river, although these are well maintained by firms who have been in the business for a considerable time. Many of the inns have the unsophisticated charm of the Broads years ago, but Fenland is really like a maiden who has to be wooed and won. The visitor who takes the trouble to explore, particularly the lesser known tributaries of the Ouse, will surely find her and be amply rewarded. Fenland will particularly appeal to the private boatowner who enjoys the East Anglian scene and the fun and friendship to be found in a boat club. The Nene in particular is a haven for the private owner on one of our least known rivers.

The flora and fauna of the Fens are of special interest. The visitor could start with *A Field Guide to the Birds of Britain and Europe,* a pocket-book published by Collins, and then go on to the *Popular Handbook of British Birds* published by

Witherby. The birds in particular represent ordinary farming country rather than those to be found in marshes and meres. Years ago there were duck decoys all over England, and it is said that they took over 5,000 birds a year. J. Wentworth Day records only five decoys left in the whole of England and Wales, of which Orwell Park Decoy in Suffolk and Fritton Lake Decoy, also in Suffolk, are the two main ones.

Those of us who visit the Fens regularly love the enormous spread of sky strung across often by wild geese. Pink-footed geese are the most numerous, and grey-lag geese are still to be seen. At night the geese are out on the marsh flats by the coast, but in the day time they come inland. The Wash is one of their favourite habitats. Keith Shackleton, the painter, generally finds the pink-footed geese his favourite choice.

Partridges and pheasants are on most Fen farms, though quail and bustards, recently quite common, seem to have disappeared. The bittern is probably the bird that stands out most in the Fens, and it has returned to nest in Wicken Fen. There are sparrowhawks and kestrels, buzzards in winter and a number of varieties of owl, and you will see herons everywhere, and several varieties of swan. The mallard is a very common duck in Wicken, and they can be seen flying sometimes a hundred at a time. There is as well the great crested and little grebe, and myriads of small birds like the reed and sedge warbler.

Amongst animals you will find the otter, the polecat, weasel, stoat, rabbit and hare, together with water rats of different varieties. Badgers have rarely been seen, doubtless due to the intensive cultivation. Those who travel by water may see an occasional porpoise in the Ouse and Nene, and the Wash is famous for its seals. The fish are legendary; numerous pike running to over fifty pound being taken in the area. The Middle Level drains have some of the finest fishing in the country—carp, dace, perch, pike and rudd are the regular fish, and there have been some enormous eels caught on occasions. The peculiar three-pronged fork called the eel gleave is the symbol on the burgee of the Middle Level Watermen's Club.

The waterman who wants to look at flora and fauna must visit Wicken Fen, a branch off Burwell Lode, and National Trust property. This section of Fen country has been left in its natural state, but this waterlogged and uncultivated area is many feet higher than the adjacent peat lands. There are over 170 species of flowering plants to be found in the Fen, and the sedge that grows in the area makes an efficient thatching material, still in great demand for houses as a capping for the reeds. There are few wild animals in the area apart from the odd fox or otter. Few frogs or toads either, and the snakes to be seen swimming across the lodes are harmless grass snakes, for the adder is unknown. Joyce V. Barnes, Resident Keeper at Wicken Fen, says that there are more than 1,075 kinds of beetle and 737 varieties of butterfly and moth in the area. A hide has been built on the sedge fen side of Wicken Lode with two telescopes for observing wildfowl, and 250 ducks of six different species have been counted at one time. A new mere has been excavated from a bequest which gives an area of open water of about ten acres. This is attracting a good number of wildfowl to the area. Here at Wicken the changes in flora and fauna in the English wetlands can be studied. Visitors to the Fen must first visit the Keeper's house and sign the visitors' book, and no collecting is allowed unless special permission has been granted. The Fen birds and animals are quite harmless to neighbouring farmers, and this helps the work of the Trust in preserving this unique piece of old Fenland. There is an excellent guide to Wicken Fen published by the National Trust, price 12½p. Incidentally, it is here that the visitor can learn something about the peat cutting that was carried out in the old Fens for fuel. There is an enormous quantity of peat still available, but very little is harvested commercially. The enthusiast could do no better than read *The History of the Fens* by J. Wentworth Day. Much more than a history, and never a dry one at that, this book is a mine of information about the wild life of the Fen country.

CHAPTER SEVEN

Cruising the Nene and Middle Level

In common with other rivers on the Fenland network, land drainage interests are paramount, and particular care should be taken to watch water levels. Occasionally, during a wet season, cruising may be held up as the guillotine gates fitted to most locks may have to be permanently raised for several days so that water may discharge itself downstream. The navigation doors as they are called in the area (incidentally, locks are frequently referred to as pens) are generally found closed, and the usual practice is to leave them closed after passing through the lock. Sometimes the slackers on the locks (paddles to the canal man) are used to control water discharge in rainy weather, and if you find a lock with one slacker fully or partly open you should leave it as you found it after locking through. Locks will often be found in a series opened in this way. If in doubt consult the River Authority by telephone.

The enthusiast should certainly read *The Black Fens* by A. K. Astbury and Professor H. C. Darby's book *The Draining of the Fens*. After reading these, and looking at the problems on site, one cannot help but marvel at the work done by the drainage authorities, and what they do to assist navigation, which, of course, is not here their most vital concern.

There are 38 locks on the Nene between Northampton and the tideway. Those from Peterborough to Northampton take craft 78ft by 13ft beam with 4ft of water, the headroom under normal conditions being 7ft 3in. Downstream from Peterborough through the large electrically operated Dog-in-a-Doublet lock craft up to 130ft long by 20ft beam with a draught of 6-7ft can navigate the river, but Guyhirne bridge does give restricted headroom. Under very high water conditions this can be as little as 4ft, but at low water ordinary neap tides there is 13ft, and providing one takes care to navigate at the right time no difficulty should be experienced.

The River Nene is a river for the enthusiast, not only pretty, with locks in excellent order, but with a total lack of commercialism. Yet those who are members of the nine clubs operating on the river find ample facilities. There are literally dozens of places where one can moor and walk to an unspoilt inn, though an inn by the riverside itself is comparatively rare.

The River Nene is only in the Fen country from Peterborough downstream, but for Fenland cruising purposes it is considered as part of the Fenland network. The Nene rises near Badby and becomes a navigation when it reaches Northampton.

There is a good deal of interest for our American friends in this area. George Washington, Benjamin Franklin and John Adams all came from Northamptonshire stock. Sulgrave Manor is well away from the Nene and beyond the scope of this book, but its associations with the Washington family are very close indeed and could be included in a tour of the area. Close by the county town is Little Brington and Great Brington. Both have close associations with the Washington family and in Great Brington church is the tomb of Laurence Washington who died in 1616. Ecton near the Nene at Cogenhoe has associations with Benjamin Franklin, whose father was a blacksmith in the village. Several of his relations are buried in the churchyard and there is a memorial in the church.

The Nene is joined at Northampton by a branch of the

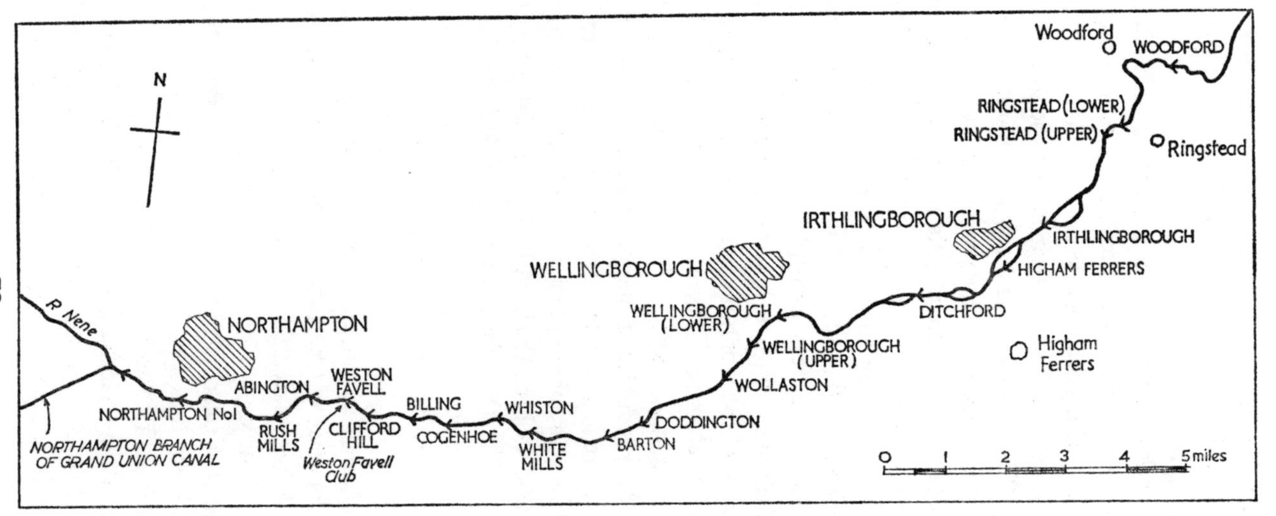

The Upper Nene

Grand Union Canal, and until recently narrow boats carrying grain traded on this branch and on to the Nene to the mills at Wellingborough.

The first lock at Northampton is situated in Becket's Park with excellent moorings close to tennis courts, bowling greens and some delightful flower gardens. Too often the waterside scene is a place which the town forgets, and the squalor in some is appalling. The tidying up and town planning that has gone on by the Avon Cosmetics Factory is well worth a look at by any student of town planning. This rivals the excellent work done on the Birmingham Canal Navigations at the Cincinnati Works. It is interesting that both these two public-spirited efforts have been undertaken by American-owned companies.

Northampton is a fast expanding town with well over 100,000 inhabitants, with a first class shopping centre and market near excellent moorings with a number of good hotels and interesting churches. There was a disastrous fire in the town in 1675 and All Saints Church was built immediately afterwards. It resembles a temple instead of an Anglican church, and there is a very fine chancel of good proportions.

It should be remembered that the first lock at Northampton and the second lock at Rush Mills have radial gates, as also does lock No 15 at Ditchford downstream. Full details of how to work these gates are supplied to hire boat users on the river, and also to visiting craft on the river when application is made for keys to the River Authority. These radial gates, which work on the principle of up and over, are not entirely popular contraptions. The rest of the locks on the river have straightforward guillotine gates rising vertically.

There is a flourishing Northampton Boat Club, and also one at the village of Weston Favell, and there are seven other clubs to be found on the river downstream—the Middle Nene Cruising Club at Titchmarsh, the Oundle Cruising Club and the Oundle Sailing Club. Then there is the Peterborough Cruising Club and the Peterborough Yacht Club near Peterborough, and in addition the Aylton Cruising Association and the Wisbech Yacht Club. These clubs have all been banded together in the Association of Nene River Clubs, an independent body formed by The East Anglian Waterways Association Ltd, who are also members of this grouping. All will help members of visiting clubs who are in difficulty.

The Britannia Inn is just below Rush Mills lock, and after these locks there is pleasant open country until Billing Aquadrome is reached by a channel just below the lock. There are moorings for visiting craft, a slipway, and many attractions for children including a funfair and miniature railway. There are also boating lakes for other waterborne activities. The place is quite unique, particularly for the holidaymaker.

The scenery of the Nene plain has an air all its own, and you feel particularly remote from the nearby villages. Cogenhoe is just below lock No 7, about half a mile from a chalet settlement by the river. Near Whitemills lock No 9 is Earls Barton village with its famous Saxon tower on the church. Castle Ashby village with Castle Ashby, the seat of the Marquess of Northampton, is approximately two miles due south of the lock. There is a good footpath through the park to the house and village.

In the section leading to Barton lock No 10 there is a wild life sanctuary, and at Doddington lock there is a magnificent specimen of a Nene mill, a photographer's delight. Water tanks can be filled here for a small fee. Near Wollaston lock, only about half a mile away, is Great Doddington village reached by a short footpath, and a good port of call at the Stags Head Inn.

Just above lock No 13, the first of the Wellingborough locks, is the River Authority's depot reached by a short channel running north; the slipway here can usually be used by special arrangement if advance notice is given. Below this lock there is a very pleasant mooring at Little Irchester near the paddling pool. There are toilets nearby which can be unlocked using your lock keys. Close by is the Cottage Inn, a port of call for bargemen until the traffic ceased recently.

Wellingborough is about a mile away. There is the excellent

Hind Hotel, and also a zoo. In spite of being an up and coming industrial town there are a number of interesting old buildings; the parish church is in the main six hundred years old and well worth a visit. John Askham, a poet who deserves to be better known, was born at Wellingborough. He died in his home which he called Clare Cottage after the better known but sad John Clare who came from Helpston near Peterborough.

Near here the largest tributary of the Nene comes in from the north bank, the River Ise, which rises near Naseby. Another unnamed tributary also rises here running through Cottesbrook Park, a delightful village in yellow Northamptonshire stone, rivalling more famous villages in the Cotswolds.

Naseby, famous for its battle of 1645, has an obelisk commemorating the event near the village, but the true site of the battle is some two miles north of the village on Broadmoor, also marked by a monument. Shakespeare's Avon rises near the battlefield.

Proceeding downstream before Higham Ferrers is one of the lowest bridges on the river needing special care, although in exceptional cases it may be possible to gain an extra inch or two of headroom by opening the paddles of the lock, but take expert local advice if necessary.

The town close by which names the lock has a fine church and buildings, and Mr J. T. Newington who runs Oundle Marina succinctly states it is reminiscent of a small cathedral town.

The next section has a tannery and sewage works on it, and after passing the two Ringstead locks the next best halt for a port of call is Woodford village across the field from the lock where the Duke's Arms Inn has excellent catering facilities. Near Denford lock is Denford village with the Cock Inn and the pleasant village of Islip with its Woolpack Inn. Islip sees occasional American visitors as the church has a monument to Mary Washington, whose husband was John Washington of Thrapston, uncle of the John Laurence Washington who sailed to America in 1657, becoming the great-grandfather of the

President. Also commemorated in the church is John Nicoll who was buried here in 1467. It was Mathias Nicoll who drew up for the Governor of New York the first copy of English laws.

The market town of Thrapston is near with a sailing club operating on a huge worked out gravel pit. Titchmarsh Mill by the lock is the headquarters of the Middle Nene Cruising Club, and near Wadenhoe lock is the lovely village of that name with the King's Head. Just below Titchmarsh is the road to Thorpe Waterville where meals can be obtained at the Fox Inn.

The woodland is particularly thick around Lilford Lock. Haunted Lilford Lock is undoubtedly the prettiest place on the river, and the section leading on to Wadenhoe rivals most other rivers. Waltheof, a Saxon lord, lived near Lilford, and although his wife was the Conqueror's niece he was put to death, and is still remembered as the first man to be beheaded in this country.

Near is the village of Pilton, which has connections with Guy Fawkes.

The two Barnwell locks either side of Oundle Marina are a series of interconnected lakes formerly gravel pits where full mooring facilities and excellent moorings are available. The only fleet of hire cruisers on the river operates from here and by arrangement it is possible to see the Fairline cruisers being made from glass fibre.

Ashton lock No 28 is a very attractive spot with a delightful mooring in the backwater. Close by is the dignified stone-built town of Oundle with its fine church and famous public school; also two good inns, the Talbot and the George. The Talbot has a staircase which is said to have come from Fotheringhay Castle.

By Cotterstock lock is the famous hall built in the sixteenth and seventeenth centuries. The village near the hall, as well as Tansor, are very attractive. The curious lock named Perio, No 30, is the last before Fotheringhay with its grand perpendicular church and lantern tower by the river. What is left is only half of what it was over five hundred years ago as the choir and college buildings were pulled down so that the lead and stones could be used elsewhere. The castle mound is all that remains of the castle where Richard III was born and Mary Queen of Scots executed. The Falcon Inn is near and care should be taken at the low bridge.

Warmington lock and village follow downstream with the Red Lion and a very fine church in the village. A pleasant section of river leads on from Elton, which has the stately home of Elton Hall, open on some occasions, and there are moorings at the Queens Head Inn reached by a short backwater. Wansford in England follows shortly, and the Paper Mills Inn here has a landing stage on the river. The Haycock Inn is in the village.

Alwalton lock, No 36, with the Peterborough Cruising Club close by, is very near to the A.1 and boats can often be slipped in from visiting clubs. By Alwalton lock is the old Mill Head stream, which is leased to Mr Leslie Critchley, Chairman of The East Anglian Waterways Association Ltd, and moorings are often available to visitors. Near the next lock at Orton is the Peterborough Yacht Club and the Windmill Inn is in the village adjacent.

Peterborough is a modern town heavily congested with traffic, but do not let this put you off from seeking out its ancient cathedral. Moorings on the town quay and sometimes the River Authority's quay may be used with permission. There are a few old buildings in the town, but the seventeenth century Guildhall and the Customs House are worth visiting.

Downstream from Peterborough the river is in a straight artificial channel, the last lock being Dog-in-a-Doublet, No 38. It is a tidal lock and power-operated. There is a free house named after the lock serving meals adjacent, and if you wish to moor here at the dolphins, ask the lock-keeper's permission to walk through his garden.

Downstream from Peterborough great care must be taken at

Page 85 (*above*) Marmount Priory Lock, Middle Level; (*below*) Well Creek near Outwell. This route is very like Holland. Middle Level.

Page 86 (*above*) New Bedford Sluice near Salters Lode. This can only be passed when tide makes a level. This route is via Welches Dam and is much longer than the Well Creek route; (*below*) Denver Sluice, River Great Ouse. On the right is the navigation lock with gates that open either way, to allow for all tidal conditions.

Guyhirne bridge which gives very little headroom under high water conditions. It must be remembered that you are now in the tideway and there are no moorings until Wisbech is reached. If you are going to make this trip you should get in touch with the Harbourmaster (Wisbech 5761) beforehand and he will assist you with mooring and pilotage across the Wash if this is required.

Usually it is best to leave the tidal lock as soon as there is sufficient depth of water on the flood tide. Wisbech is an old Fenland town. In the Castle here King John heard the sad news that his jewels had been lost in the Wash; the castle has gone, but on the site is an excellent museum. There is an ancient church of St Peter and St Paul with three nave arcades, and some interesting buildings to be found in this bustling town. It is also a centre of the canning industry.

Downstream Sutton bridge is reached. Here there is a special pontoon which is owned by the Association of Nene River Clubs as an emergency mooring in a very difficult part of the river. The 'Big Tom' beacon to starboard marks the end of the river channel. The intrepid navigator will want to explore the Middle Level. This is under another Authority, the Middle Level Commissioners. To navigate the Nene you will have applied to the Welland & Nene River Authority and paid your dues, and obtained lock keys and instructions. The keys unlock the fixed windlasses, but on the Middle Level ordinary windlasses are required and up to date instructions must be sought from the Engineer's office.

The Middle Level

Leaving Peterborough there is a short channel to starboard under the twin arched wooden railway bridge, which leads on to Stanground Creek, and there are in fact two boatyards here. This Creek leads to Stanground lock. Those wishing to make the trip must give forty-eight hours' notice to the Middle Level Commissioners at March. The commissioners will issue bye-laws and information to assist navigators. If possible, fourteen days' notice will give even greater assistance.

It has to be remembered that the Middle Level, the area between the Nene and the Ouse, is at a lower level than the two rivers it joins. Craft lock down into the Middle Level and then up again out of it. This is due to the slow sinkage of the Black Fens caused by the draining and pumping operations over very many years.

You can get into the system at three points—Ashline Lock at Whittlesey; Horseway Lock at the end of the Forty Foot River, or via Priory Lock just near the north end of the Twenty Foot River. The route via Well Creek and Priory Lock is going to be reopened in the near future, and as we go to press repairs are being made to Priory Lock. This is by far the most suitable route through the Level. The other route via Welches Dam is entered from the Old Bedford River. To get into the Old Bedford River it is necessary to go through the tidal doors at Salter's Lode when the ebb tide makes a level. The Old Bedford River to Welches Dam Lock and through to Horseway is under the jurisdiction of the Great Ouse River Authority. The route through can be via March or Benwick.

For a newcomer to the area, help can usually be arranged by Mr L. Critchley, 36 Waterloo Road, Peterborough, who being closely connected with East Anglian and Fenland waterway affairs for many years is in a position to give advice and help to visitors. Club members are recommended to get in touch with the Middle Level Watermen's Club who have moorings by the bridge in March by the old course of the River Nene, and who have been very hospitable to travellers through the Level with advice and help. Leslie Heaton and Fred Simons of this club know the area intimately.

There is a boatyard at March, but no hire cruisers will be found in the Level except under special circumstances. Oundle Marina, the only yard on the River Nene which hires out craft, will under certain circumstances allow very experienced owners to take craft into the Level, and similarly, Appleyard Lincoln at Ely have been equally helpful. Naturally, commercial operators need to know something of the credentials of those who want to navigate the difficult stretches which need the maximum initiative. Craft need to be not more than 10ft 9in beam, and the maximum headroom is 6ft, although sometimes there is an inch or two to spare at Welches Dam. The floor of Stanground Lock is higher than the upper sill of Ashline Lock, and usually 2ft 6in is the maximum draught that can be taken through, although there are some enthusiasts who have got 2ft 9in through from the Nene to the Ouse. Strictly speaking, the locks being 46ft long, it should be possible to get a boat 46ft by 10ft 9in through the Level, but the very narrow river section and tight corner at Whittlesey does in fact limit craft to about 35ft. Much depends upon the type of boat; a narrow beamed, shortened narrow boat 46ft long with 6ft 10in beam only has successfully navigated the difficult section. It is $4\frac{1}{4}$ miles from Whittlesey Village to Stanground Lock, and then just over 6 miles to Floods Ferry, the junction with the old Nene River. From Floods Ferry through March to Outwell is just over 13 miles, and from Outwell to Salter's Lode Lock is nearly $5\frac{1}{2}$ miles.

In the Fen country it is usual to refer to locks as sluices, and further confusion can arise at Salter's Lode where there is a lock with doors which work both ways leading into Well Creek, at present unnavigable, and there is also the Old Bedford Sluice nearby, which has tidal doors which are only used on the ebb tide. The expression locally is not to lock a boat through, but to pen it through, and locks are often referred to as pens.

The Middle Level has many miles of straight drainage channels with high banks, and it would need a very dyed in the wool enthusiast to appreciate them, but there are sections of the Middle Level with high amenity value. Through Upwell and Outwell the area reflects the interest of the Dutch drainage engineers, and is strongly reminiscent of Holland. The old River Nene through March is extremely attractive, particularly on the north side of the bridge in the town by a small inn called the Ship. On the south side of the bridge is the club headquarters with the only mooring locally available and an extremely good inn, the White Horse, with a landing stage with a fine Norfolk reed thatched roof. Students of Victoriana in architecture might like to add March Town Hall to their list, which rivals in many ways the obelisk in St Ives market place. There is also the pretty village of Benwick, famous amongst other things for its houses leaning at all angles due to the shrinkage of the peat following drainage schemes.

There is a most interesting Nature Reserve at Woodwalton Fen. This consists of 514 acres 8 miles south east of Peterborough, on Raveley Drain. Much work has been undertaken to keep a high water level during the year and clear the woody vegetation which had encroached when the area was dry. The Reserve is rich in plant and animal life, which has disappeared elsewhere as the Fens have been drained. A permit is required to visit, but this is given to serious students if application is made to the Nature Conservancy at Bracondale, Norwich.

The expression Isle of Ely is often mentioned in connection with this area, and this will be dealt with in the Ouse section, but the towns of Chatteris, March and Whittlesey stand on their own islands like Ely. The towns were built on whatever high ground was available as the surrounding country was Fen, and in days gone by were virtually little islands.

There is not very much left of the Abbey at Ramsey, although part of the gateway remains. The church near was probably built from much of the stones of the Abbey. The intrepid Middle Level traveller could well take notice of the inscription over the west door in the tower which reads 'Take heed watch and pray for ye know not what the time is'.

The entry or exit from the old River Nene is a straightforward one, though you must wait for the ebb tide on the Old Bedford route, the only one generally available as this book goes to press. Some small craft have been able to get through the Well Creek route and Salter's Lode Lock.

Leaving by either route from the Middle Level you are then in the tideway of the Great Ouse. If you wish to go up the New Bedford River to Earith, you may have to wait for a young flood tide; otherwise it is necessary to go through Denver Sluice (lock) and the Ely Ouse. The beginner should be wary of trying to force his way against the ebb tide up the New Bedford, it takes much longer than one would think and you may find insufficient draught above Mepal.

The vital thing to remember in the Middle Level is that levels are all important. The lock-keepers at Stanground and also at Salter's Lode are extremely helpful as well as the general foreman of the Middle Level. When levels are low there is shoaling by pumping stations. There are no lock charges at the present moment, but the services of lock-keepers always merit a gratuity, though the Fenlander is a proud man, and not tip-hungry.

The Middle Level gives you very deserted waterways, except when the fishermen from the Midlands and industrial North are in evidence. They descend on the drains in vast numbers, but local inquiries will enable you to avoid clashes with their fishing matches. There is some of the finest coarse fishing in the country to be found in these long, lonely drains.

If you are a stranger to this part of the country, remember when you are mooring up that the breezes are much stronger. The fine bracing air will make you much hungrier, so make sure ample stores are aboard.

The map will show you that the routes through the Middle Level can be varied, and March and Benwick should certainly be added to the list. Like March, there are several good inns at Benwick. In fact there are a surprising number of inns scattered throughout the Middle Level, all of them with reasonable moorings, but they are not well charted. There is even a small beer house near Welches Dam to relieve the monotony of the Old Bedford, and there is another, the Three Tuns, at Welney. Those who have navigated the area have found the Griffin at March a useful port of call as it is an inn serving luncheons and dinners in an area not particularly endowed with such facilities. A feature of the Middle Level is the *Shell Fen,* a small oil tanker operated by Mr Lincoln to deliver fuel to pumping stations.

There is an excellent strip map of the River Nene from Northampton to Peterborough, compiled and drawn for Oundle Marina by W. S. Williamson, and this can be obtained from Imray, Laurie, Norie & Wilson Ltd, Wych House, St Ives, Hunts, or ordered through any bookshop. This gives ample details for a cruise for the 65 miles from Northampton to Dog-in-a-Doublet Lock.

DISTANCE TABLES

	miles	*fur*
River Nene		
Northampton, junction with Northampton branch of the Grand Union Canal, to:		
Northampton, South Bridge		1
Wellingborough Bridge	12	7
Irthlingborough Bridge	18	1
Thrapston Bridge	26	1
Oundle Bridge	38	0
Wansford Bridge	49	5
Peterborough Bridge	60	5
Junction with branch to Stanground and Middle Level Navigations	61	1
Dog-in-a-Doublet Lock	65	5
Wisbech Town Bridge	79	6
Sutton Bridge	87	3
The Wash at Crabs Hole, mouth of river	91	4
Middle Level Navigation (River Nene to River Ouse)		
Head of Stanground Sluice (Lock) and junction with Stanground branch of River Nene, called Broadwater, to:		
Kings Dyke		
Fields End Bridge	2	2
Whittlesey Village, junction with Whittlesey Dyke	4	2

	miles	*fur*
Whittlesey Dyke		
Whittlesey or Ashline Sluice (Lock)	4	5½
Angle Corner, junction with Twenty-foot River (navigable) and Bevil's Leam	7	0
Floods Ferry, junction with Old River Nene	10	3
Staffurth's Bridge	11	3
March	15	3
Twenty-foot End, junction with Twenty-foot River	17	4½
Popham's Eau End, junction with Popham's Eau	19	4
Marmont Priory Sluice (Lock)	21	2
Upwell	22	4
Outwell, junction with Well Creek	23	2
Well Creek		
Aqueduct over Middle Level Drain	24	4
Nordelph	26	5
Salter's Lode Sluice (Lock), and junction with River Ouse	28	5

From Angle Corner, there is an alternative route by Bevil's Leam and the Old Nene River to Floods Ferry

Bevil's Leam		
Chapelbridge	1	4½
Pondersbridge	3	5
Tebbit's Bridge	4	4
Mere Mouth, junction with Old River Nene and Black Ham Drain (navigable)	5	0
Old River Nene		
Exhibition Bridge	7	4
Nightingale's Corner, junction with New Dyke (navigable)	7	6
St Mary's village and bridge	8	4
Saunders Bridge, junction with Ramsey High Lode	10	6
Wells Bridge, junction with Forty-foot River (navigable)	11	5
Benwick village and bridge	15	5
Floods Ferry, junction with Whittlesey Dyke	18	2

(For full details of the Middle Level Navigation, see Lewis A. Edwards, *Inland Waterways of Great Britain and Ireland.*)

CHAPTER EIGHT

Cruising the Great Ouse and its Tributaries

Bedford to Tempsford

The navigation of the Ouse begins at Bedford Bridge, although it appears there is a prescriptive right of navigation for some distance above the bridge. Bedford is Bunyan's town, famous for its schools. There are four fine churches for the visitor to see, relics of Bunyan, and associations with John Howard, the great prison reformer. Bedford is a fine town by the River Ouse, and the promenade by the river thrusts a green finger through the centre of the town. But, alas, for too long Bedford has been isolated from the waterway system by the dereliction of its locks. The Great Ouse Restoration Society was formed in 1951, and has raised money to assist the river authority and its predecessors to rebuild navigation structures. Bedford Town Lock, No 1, and Cardington Lock, No 2 have both been put into working order, and the Society is in the process of raising £5,000 to assist with the rebuilding of Roxton Lock above Tempsford. This done, four more derelict locks will remain, Barford Lock, Old Mills Lock, Willington Lock and Castle Lock, between Roxton and Cardington. These four need to be rebuilt to link the Bedford end with the rest of the navigable River Great Ouse. Plans have been put forward by the river authority for reconstructing these locks, to go ahead when finances permit. The river can be navigated for light craft from Roxton upstream from Bedford if they can be portaged around the lock structures. There is a map of the Bedford to Roxton section published by Imray, Laurie, Norie & Wilson Ltd, Wych House, St Ives, Hunts, and they also publish a map of the main River Great Ouse called *The Enclosed Waters of the Rivers Cam & Great Ouse.* The whole of the river and its tributaries is under the control of the Great Ouse River Authority with the exception of the River Cam from Bottisham Lock to Cambridge, which is controlled by the Conservators of the River Cam. Lock reconstruction was commenced by the Great Ouse Catchment Board before the last war, and work was continued by the Great Ouse River Board and its successor, the Great Ouse River Authority. The lock sizes on the Ouse tend to vary, but they are generally about 100ft long and 10ft 6in wide.

The highest point cruisers coming up the river can at present reach is the Anchor Hotel at Tempsford, which is above the Great North Road bridge, and just below this on the journey to the sea are the remains of Tempsford Staunch. This is an old flash lock, a direct descendant of those old single gate locks so very wasteful of water which were used on our rivers before the introduction of the pound lock. Remains of this type of staunch can be found in several places on East Anglian waterways. As we go to press, Roxton Lock is being built. Navigation will then be possible upwards to just below the lock at Great Barford, where there is an attractive village with its inn and church by the river.

Tempsford to Popes Corner

From Tempsford the river is pleasantly wooded to Eaton Socon, where there is a lock. The village adjacent has a delightful village green, a fine church and a pleasant old inn which has associations with Charles Dickens, the inn featuring in Nicholas Nickleby. The church is especially interesting, having been built in our time to replace the old one destroyed

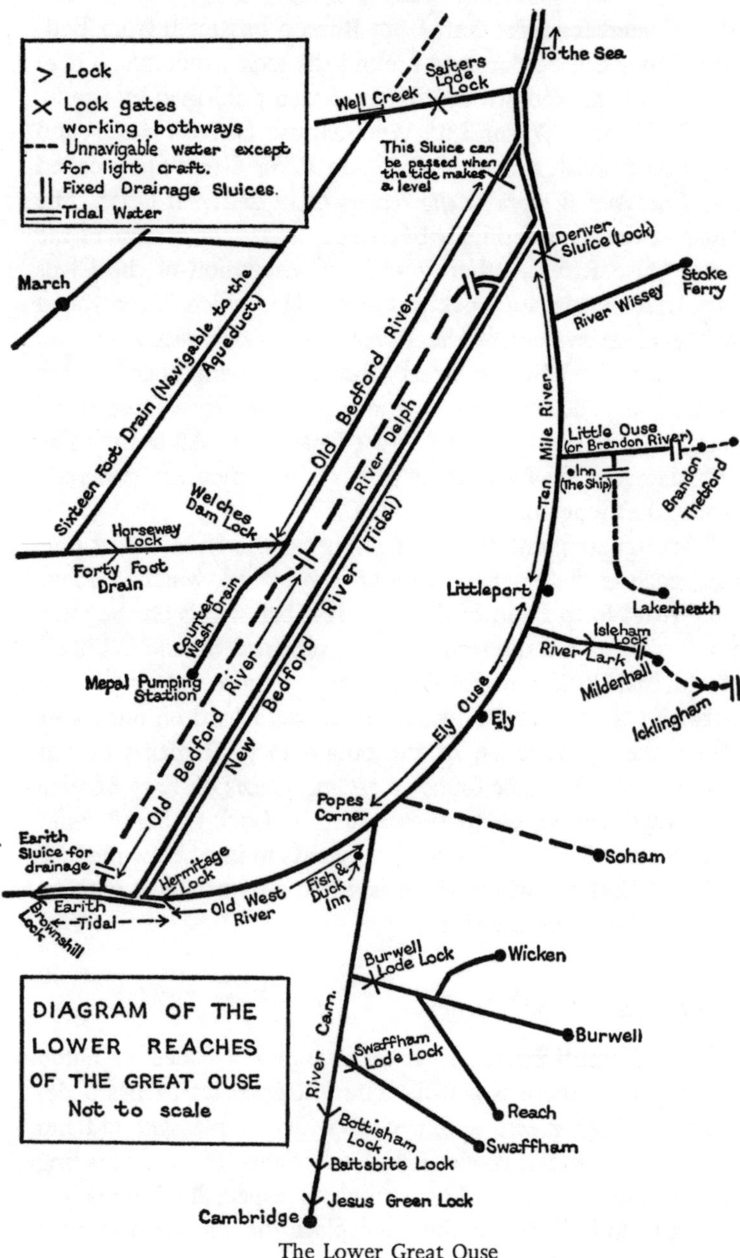

The Lower Great Ouse

by fire. There are no boatyard facilities here, Kelpie Marine Yard at Tempsford being the only one on this stretch of river until St Neots is reached. Here there is a fine bridge, and the market place has some good inns around it. St Neots is lucky and famous for still having its own brewery, the normal thing for most English country towns in the past. Like Southwold in Suffolk you can enjoy a good brew of reasonably priced ale produced locally. The church is often called Huntingdonshire's cathedral. St Neots is the home of the Ouse Valley River Club. A. R. Brearley runs a boatyard which operates from a mooring south of the river, and near is the White House Club, which has its own boat club operating from the boatyard. The Bridge Hotel and the Cross-keys are well used by river men. Fleming Holidays Afloat operates from Brearley's boatyard.

Downstream is the well known Paper Mill Lock, notorious for shallowness. Although it has been deepened in recent years, care is still undoubtedly needed. The charts should be carefully followed to avoid shoals below the lock. For the intrepid, the River Kym, just above the lock can usually be navigated for about a mile. Pleasant wooded country follows Offord Lock, and nearby at Buckden Mr W. B. Carter has an excellent laid out mooring and boatyard. It is considered by many to be a model of its type. The work of Mr Carter for waterways has stood out for a long time, and those who navigate the river owe him a debt of gratitude.

Next come Offord Cluny and Offord Darcy, once lacemaking centres, which have now reverted to two charming villages with pleasant river scenery, particularly by the mill and weir. A further attractive stretch of river follows to Brampton Lock, by the small village with associations with Samuel Pepys. It is a short distance to Godmanchester, which was made a borough in 1212. The north side of the river is Huntingdon; recently, Huntingdon and Godmanchester having been linked together, they were given a new Charter.

Godmanchester is a beautiful spot to linger in, with old

houses round the river backwaters. There is a very fine lattice-work bridge, called the Chinese bridge, which looks for all the world as if it has just jumped off a willow pattern plate. There is an old town hall and Elizabethan school, and a very old bridge which links Godmanchester to Huntingdon. Cruisers can be hired from the Bridge Boatyard at Huntingdon.

Huntingdon has associations dating back before Roman times. Cromwell was born here and was educated at the grammar school, and some of the Norman buildings of the school are still in existence. Cowper, the poet, lived in the town for some time. There are a number of fine Georgian buildings and an inn by the river which was the scene of many early meetings about Fen waterway matters; much of the voluntary work in the area was planned in this building. Another popular inn is the George with its lovely old courtyard. There are numerous other inns in the back streets and first class facilities for the visitor. The Falcon Inn, a very old building in Market Square by the George, has always welcomed visitors to the river, and for many years now East Anglian Waterway Association Ltd meetings have been held here. Oddly enough, Cromwell's statue is to be found in St Ives, and the general view seems to be that Huntingdon did not want it, although the town did make some amends by putting a stone in 1938 by the Norman doorway of the school. This is the town's only memorial to Cromwell. All Saints Church looks over towards the cobbled courtyard of the Falcon, and St Mary's is also of great interest. Nearby is Hinchingbrooke, with its Cromwellian associations, and although it suffered badly from fire in 1830, it has been well rebuilt. Elysian Holidays Ltd has its hire cruiser base at Huntingdon, situated at the old Childs & Hall boatyard, accommodating also its fleet previously operating at Ely. The boats are based upon the Elysian fibreglass hull manufactured by Appleyard, Lincoln (Boabuilders) of Ely.

Downstream from Huntingdon is a marina with full facilities on the north bank at Hartford. Nearby is the headquarters of the Hunts Sailing Club.

Some 6 miles north of here is Monks Wood, totalling 387 acres, of which 370 are woodland. The reserve is a classic locality for rare insects, the most famous being the Black Hairstreak butterfly, which was first discovered in Britain in 1828. There are a number of plants that are rare in East Anglia, and some very fine trees. A permit from the East Anglia Region of the Nature Conservancy at Norwich is required to visit it.

Above and below the next lock at Houghton are a number of backwaters, most of them very narrow. Huntingdon is $2\frac{3}{4}$ miles away, and St Neots nearly 13. Houghton Mill, mentioned in Domesday Book and, of course, very famous, was restored by the local people and presented to the Council for the Protection of Rural England and used as a Youth Hostel. It is now owned by the National Trust.

Near to this is Hutson's Boatyard, a small but useful and friendly organisation. Below Houghton Lock is one of the most photographed stretches of the river by Hemingford Grey church, and here rowing boats can be hired from the boathouse. Hemingford Grey and the adjoining Hemingford Abbots have picturesque houses and churches. Canal enthusiasts will be intrigued to be reminded that John Gunning and his four beautiful daughters came to Hemingford Grey from Ireland; Maria and Elizabeth entered London society and Elizabeth became attached to Francis, Duke of Bridgewater; but fortunately for the canal era the affair did not last long.

Below the next lock at Hemingford is a lovely stretch of water very popular with sailing clubs and motor cruisers who take appropriate avoiding action. Then comes St Ives with its famous bridge and interesting old buildings and inns. The bridge is truly a magnificent structure with its chantry chapel in the centre, dedicated to St Leger; there is a good local museum and first class mooring above and below the bridge. The backwater around the Waits is shallow. St Ives with its beautiful church is really the gateway to the Fens. Its fifteenth century nave is particularly good. One of the books kept in an old chest in the church has Cromwell's signature in it as churchwarden. Years ago St Ive was known as Slepe when he did missionary work here, and there is a local hostelry called Slepe Hall recalling this fact. If you take the trouble to seek out its nooks and crannies and alleyways the town is well worth a visit. Some vision, perhaps a face lift by the Civic Trust, could work wonders with St Ives.

Downstream from St Ives is Laurie Jones' boatyard which has full marina facilities at the Boathaven. Hire craft also operate from here. Below St Ives lock there is the old ferry crossing of Hereward the Wake, and the small village of Holywell. From St Ives Bridge, Holywell is 3 miles, and to Huntingdon just over 5½ miles. The Ferry Boat Inn is said to have existed in part as long ago as 980. Here is one of Fenland's ghost stories. Juliet Tewsley took her life after a bout of unrequited love for a local woodcutter. She died on 17 March 1050; her gravestone, a slab of grey granite, is incorporated in the inn floor, and Juliet's ghost is said to walk each year from the stone in the inn floor on St Patrick's Day. There is a good inn, the Pike & Eel, downstream with a boat club operating from here with the same name, and below is Brownshill Staunch (a lock of course), just over 5 miles from St Ives Lock. Below Brownshill the Ouse is tidal right down to the New Bedford River to Denver and out to sea, but the New Bedford route is seldom used. Brownshill Staunch is the beginning of a wooded section of river, almost the last for many miles.

Earith has good moorings at the Crown Inn and there are full boatyard facilities and a fleet of hire boats at Fred Carrington's boatyard. If you wish to leave Earith for the New Bedford passage through to King's Lynn it is best to leave one hour before high water at Lynn. Most cruising visitors will go below Earith and lock through at Hermitage Lock into the Old West River. The Old West River from Earith through to Popes Corner is just over 11½ miles from Earith. By Twenty Pence Bridge is the Bridge Inn and by Stretham Bridge the Royal Oak. Also en route is the building housing the old Boulton & Watt beam engine near Stretham. This can be visited by special arrangement as the engine is to be preserved. The boatyard at the beginning of the Old West just below Hermitage Lock was the only facility on this route until you reach the Fish & Duck Inn at Popes Corner, the junction with the River Cam, but it is at present closed.

River Cam

The Cam is the largest tributary of the Ouse in this area. It is nearly 14 miles from Popes Corner to Cambridge, and nearly seven miles to the first of the three locks at Bottisham. There are two more just below Cambridge at Baitsbite and Jesus.

Coming upstream from Popes Corner, after passing through Dimmocks Cote Bridge, there is the little settlement of Upware. Here there is a lock with an electrically operated guillotine gate and pointing doors working either way that gives entrance to Burwell and Reach Lodes. It is possible to get to Reach village, a small, sleepy hamlet, once famous for heavy barge traffic, and so important that it held a large annual fair under royal patronage. The other lode leads through the Fens to Burwell village with a church and castle mound having associations with King Stephen of the twelfth century. The Anchor Inn has a mooring at Burwell, although the lode does tend to be shallow at the top end. Leading off northwards from Burwell Lode, after passing under a small wooden bridge is Wicken Fen, a most important Nature Reserve, full of rare animals and insects. It is controlled by the National Trust, and it is possible to visit this Nature Reserve by boat, as there are good moorings at the head of the navigation.

Upstream from the entrance to the lock near Upware is Bottisham Lock, and this, like the other three locks, is under the control of the Cam Conservancy, whose jurisdiction begins at this lock. Remember a separate registration is required for the Cam. The river and tributaries below here give very good cruising between Bottisham and Hermitage Sluice near Earith,

Denver on the main river and the Wissey and Brandon River, the total being over sixty miles of lock-free water.

Above Bottisham Lock is the headquarters of the Cambridge Motor Boat Club, one of the premier clubs in the area, and between Bottisham and the next lock at Baitsbite the earthworks of the Caer Dyke constructed by the Romans can be seen in the fields between the Cam and Waterbeach. There is a good inn near the Cam Conservancy depot by Waterbeach Station. Care should be taken with sailing craft, as this stretch of river is the home of the Cam Sailing Club.

Above Baitsbite Lock Cambridge University and Town Rowing Boat Clubs use the river and care should be taken in passing the eights. There is a change of river rule for river passing notified on boards in this area near the Plough Inn at Fen Ditton. This is a favourite place for undergraduates from Cambridge and it is geared to their needs. The nosh du jour is both reasonable and satisfying, and the atmosphere accordingly bright and cheerful, unlike that so often found in places where the menus are written in bad French. There is another Pike & Eel Inn as the river enters Cambridge. H. C. Banham Ltd operates an excellent hire business and boatyard facilities here at Pye-Banham Marina. Above Jesus Lock the river winds round the famous Backs past Queens' College, King's College, Clare College, Trinity Hall, Trinity College and St John's College. The navigation ceases at the mill pond just above Silver Street Bridge. Power craft are asked not to go above Town Quay by Magdalene Bridge by Magdalene College, and legislation may be enacted to make this a statutory requirement. If navigation above the bridge is permited, the Backs should only be navigated at under 2 mph in the very early morning or late evening, otherwise the beauty of the trip will be lost.

Nobody seems to know why or in fact for certain when Cambridge started becoming a University town. Undoubtedly, a lot of trade flowed down the rivers to Cambridge, which was a trading post on the way from East Anglia to London, but it

Page 103 (*above*) Chinese bridge, Godmanchester, River Great Ouse; (*below*) Titchmarsh Lock, River Nene, headquarters of the Middle Nene Cruising Club. Taken at the Rally of the Association of River Nene Clubs 1968.

Page 104 (*above*) Lilford Lock, River Nene; (*below*) typical Fenland Marina, Buckden.

is known for certain that Peterhouse was founded in 1281, and the other colleges were formed in continuous succession from that date. You can wander round Cambridge in and out of the colleges, into the halls and chapels extremely easily, though it is well to ask for permission which, if convenient, is always freely given. The ideal way to visit Cambridge is by boat, for the town is a motorist's nightmare.

Cambridge has many links with New England. Emmanuel, which is well known as being a puritan college, assisted settlements in the United States by sending them many famous sons. John Harvard sailed to America in 1620, but died at an early age, giving half of his belongings and books to launch Harvard College. In the library of Jesus there is a copy of the first edition of the Bible which was printed in the States at Cambridge, Mass. A copy is here because the translator into the Mohican language was a man from Jesus College who tried to convert the Red Indians. The American War Cemetery here draws many people from the United States.

Christ's has famous gardens, Magdalene has the Pepys library, St John's is the second largest college, with a magnificent roof in the hall dating mostly from Tudor times. Trinity is the largest college in Cambridge, and so many great men came from here that it is impossible to list them all. Henry VIII founded this college of the Holy and Undivided Trinity just before he died in January 1547. Prime ministers, and poets, Dryden, Byron, Macaulay, Housman; scientists, Rutherford, Newton; men of letters, G. M. Trevelyan and Lord Acton; musicians, Vaughan Williams, are just a few of the famous who have passed through this ancient place. King's College has the chapel which takes the voices of the Fen country throughout the Commonwealth every Christmas in its Festival of Nine Lessons and Carols. Indeed, Cambridge needs not a week but at least a fortnight to see a little of it, but cruising by water we are able to see something not seen by the landlubber. It is possible to hire boats at Scudamore's boatyard the other side of the Backs and take a rowing boat to Grantchester, so named because the Cam above Cambridge is called the Granta. Grantchester delighted Byron and Tennyson as well as Rupert Brooke, and it is still possible to moor the boat and have honey for tea in Rupert Brooke's village. Not far from Cambridge is the ladies' college of Girton.

The Lower Ouse and its tributaries

Returning now to Popes Corner and continuing downstream we come to Ely, 14½ miles from Earith, cathedral city, one of the finest in Britain with its lantern tower. There is the Bishop's Palace and many parts of old monastic buildings which have been incorporated into King's School. Numerous fascinating old houses add to the interest of Ely.

The moorings for a visit to the city above and below the Cutter Inn at Ely are probably the finest in East Anglia; nearby is the boatyard of Appleyard, Lincoln, with a complete range of boatyard and chandlery facilities. The Cutter should be a port of call for Broadsmen holidaying in the Fens, as L. S. D. Rich (Sid) presided over the Wherry on Oulton Broad for many years. Ely has a bright and cheery air and a very obvious desire to please. (There is no Slepe here!)

A short distance below Ely is the Great Ouse River Authority depot, and also the Ely Sugar Beet factory, which in more enlightened times received sugar by barge. Downstream from Ely it is nearly 16½ miles to Denver Sluice and the beginning of the main tideway.

In the section before Denver the river has been considerably shortened as it took a long route round Prickwillow in the old days before the cut was made in 1827. Littleport is 10¼ miles below Ely, where the old railway dock is used as a marina, with the Black Horse Inn nearby. There is the Ship Inn at the junction of Brandon Creek downstream, and after passing through Hilgay Fen, Denver Sluice is reached. This is the key to the drainage of the whole of the Fens in the area. Much of the charm in this district is to be found in the tributaries which run off this section of the Ely Ouse, the River Wissey, the River Lark and the Brandon River.

The Lark is a pretty river, but leads practically nowhere, although it is hoped all cruising enthusiasts will go through Isleham Lock. You can go above Judes Ferry, but beyond that the river shallows. The inn at Judes Ferry has been closed. Above the head of navigation at the ferry there are a number of disused locks through to Bury St Edmunds, and the canoeist who attempts the trip will be surprised to find above Mildenhall a lock at Icklingham in working order, although isolated. A further lock upstream was similarly rebuilt before the last war, but no gates were ever fitted. The rate of flow in the river and the amount of abstraction in the area, plus the lowering of the twin track road over the river at Barton Mills, has made any attempt at possible restoration completely hopeless. Canoeists should certainly attempt it as the pretty woodland from Mildenhall to Bury is quite enchanting. A trip up Tuddenham mill stream can also be attempted as this was once part of the navigation.

Brandon Creek commences at the Ship. Above this inn there are a number of old staunches, or single-gated locks which used to regulate the navigation to Thetford. These have been demolished, but there is a good depth of water as far as Wilton Bridge. Navigation is uncertain above here, but when the water is reasonably high there is usually 2ft 6in of draught above Brandon Railway Bridge. It is difficult to moor here, but it is worth while trying and then forcing a path on foot to the adjacent village of Brandon. Some local clearance below Brandon Staunch and provision of a footpath to the village would be a help. Near here are Grimes Graves, the famous prehistoric mines where Neolithic man excavated his armaments. There is good water for a dinghy through to Thetford, and a lovely trip through the woods from Brandon.

Thetford is an ancient and attractive small country town, and although it has had an overspill scheme from London, at present not too much damage has been done. Little remains of the great Priory of our Lady north of the town. There are a number of other monastic remains in Thetford, the best being the old Priory founded 800 years ago by Roger Bigood. The excavations which remain are under the control of the Department of the Environment. Of the twenty parish churches which existed in Thetford, only three remain—St Mary's, St Peter's and St Cuthbert's. The best is St Mary's, although St Peter's has a good west door rebuilt nearly 200 years ago. St Cuthbert's is in the main a modern building. It is surprising that Thetford sees so few visitors from the United States, although a number of servicemen stationed in the area from that country have discovered it. The interest is Thomas Paine, commemorated by a brilliant statue situated in front of King's House. Paine was born at Thetford on the 29 January 1737, a Quaker, who went to the American Colonies in 1774. He had great influence in the American Revolution, and after a number of journeyings between the States and France, died in America in 1809. The Thomas Paine Society of the United States presented the statue to the town. He was a controversial figure, and perhaps not the best friend of the British government. Thetford has not forgotten one of the world's greatest free thinkers.

The River Wissey leaves the main river just over a mile upstream from Denver Sluice, and is navigable to just above Stoke Ferry Bridge, a distance of a little over ten miles. The river is narrow, but there is plenty of water. Hilgay is a pleasant village with good moorings two miles up river, and upstream from Hilgay there is another sugar beet factory at Wissington. This used to have a famous light railway connecting it with the sugar beet areas. Above Wissington the river widens out into a broad, but it is essential to keep to the river channel in the centre. There is woodland on the upper reaches of the river, and good moorings at the Bull with the village near. There is an intimacy about the Wissey which somehow makes people return to it time and again. An abundance of wild life exists in this area; particularly the bird life flourishes on this river, doubtless attracted by the large sheet of water above Wissington.

On the Great Ouse there are a great number of moorings in towns and villages, some at nearby hostelries, but there can be a shortage in the summer. The Great Ouse Boating Association controls some moorings on the river in certain places, reserved for members only. A number of river users find it worth while to subscribe to this organisation in order to use these moorings as do some hire cruiser operators. Care should be taken at all times in the tidal sections, and particularly in the tideway. Many readers of this book will not use the river below Denver Sluice, and those who do will need to be very well acquainted with the tidal problems regarding mooring in King's Lynn. Hire boats cannot come as far as this. Those used to navigating tidal waters who know how to use their tide table, should visit Lynn, a town bustling with prosperity, to which come coastal craft with goods mainly for the Midlands. Lynn is an old town coming to terms with the modern age. There are a number of very fine buildings in the town, St George's Guildhall, a theatre from before the days of Shakespeare, St Margaret's Church, a very fine, much photographed Customs House by the river, a wealth of Georgian houses for the merchants of the town. Lynn has a famous Festival, presided over by the very energetic Lady Fermoy, which once a year brings a cultural feast to this, one of the most attractive of English towns. The Tuesday and Saturday market places are particularly fine, the former has the Duke's Head Hotel, built by Henry Bell who also built the Customs House. John Seymour, who wrote *The Companion Guide to East Anglia* (1970), which should accompany everyone on his East Anglian travels, draws atention to the lavish use of stone at Lynn where there is no local stone to be quarried, and points out that this has come down the Nene through the Middle Level and down the Great Ouse in Fen lighters. Alas, only a few of these remain now in use by the river Authority. King's Lynn must have given many American servicemen from nearby Sculthorpe their first taste of England. It is not surprising that a number of them come back with their children, not now young, as the war is fast becoming only a memory to the veteran. Time flies as one gets older, but in Lynn it can often stand still.

The Wash

The Wash obviously is not an inland waterway, but as a tidal area it does link a number of the rivers together, and it is in the news at regular intervals in connection with the Wash Barrage Scheme. If carried out, this will make a number of differences to the inland waterway navigator travelling from the Fens to the Broads via the sea and other routes. There have been suggestions that the Wash should be dammed for very many years. In 1751 Nathaniel Kinderley produced a scheme for a dam also carrying a highway to run from King's Lynn to Boston. The depth of water in the Wash rules out putting a barrage from Skegness to Hunstanton, and also at present from Boston to King's Lynn. Comparisons with what has been done in the Netherlands must take into account that the depth of water and conditions are very different. The present suggestions are to construct four reservoirs in the Wash from pumped sandbanks. It is considered that it would cost £140 million to produce a scheme that will give 440 million gallons of fresh water a day. The problems of the Wash Barrage are going to be the subject of a £2 million study, which has recently been initiated by the Department of the Environment.

For the cruising man at the present time there is a pressing need for information about cruising the Wash. The vital facts do not seem to have been given in any publication, and therefore the author is very greatly indebted to Mr Leslie Critchley, chairman of The East Anglian Waterways Association Ltd, who comments upon the Wash area as follows:

> This is a sea area into which the rivers Welland, Witham, Nene and Great Ouse flow. It offers a sea link between

these rivers, but this route is only suitable for craft capable of some off-shore work. Narrow beam craft with a lot of top hamper should not attempt to cross the Wash unless they are compelled and have sought local advice. The tides run fast in the channels which are well buoyed and lit, but this area abounds in sand banks which change from year to year and in some places more frequently than that. The tides rise to 25ft at Springs and even on a fine day, when the tide turns against the wind a nasty short chop develops where an hour before it has been quite calm. To the experienced yachtsman a landfall in the Wash is no more difficult to make than any other, but those of lesser experience should seek advice from the Authorities or members of local river clubs when planning to cross the Wash. Members of local clubs are willing to escort or pilot boats if times are convenient. There are also a number of fishermen and retired pilots who are willing to do a trip for a fee.

DISTANCE TABLES

River Great Ouse

Bedford Bridge to:	*miles*	*fur*
Cardington	2	0
Great Barford	7	2
Tempsford Bridge	10	2
Eaton Socon	13	7
St Neots	15	0
Offord Cluny	20	1
Brampton	23	1
Godmanchester	24	3
Huntingdon	25	1
St Ives	30	6
Holywell	33	4
Earith village	38	0
Earith (route commences via New Bedford River to Denver)	38	4
Tail of Denver Sluice	58	6

	miles	*fur*
Salter's Lode, Junction with Well Creek	59	1
Downham Bridge	60	1
Kings Lynn	72	6
The Wash, mouth of river	74	6

The usual route for cruisers going downstream is, however, not by the long, straight New Bedford River as above, but by the Old West River. This leaves the tideway at Earith and locks down to the old route by Ely.

Old West River and Ely route

Earith, junction with main line of river, to:

Aldreth Bridge	3	3
Stretham Ferry	8	6
Popes Corner, junction with River Cam	11	5
Elysian Boatyard and the Cutter Inn, Ely	14	4
Junction with River Lark, navigable to Judes Ferry, 12 miles	18	6
Littleport Bridge	20	7
Brandon Creek, junction with Little Ouse	24	2
Hilgay Bridge	28	0
Junction with River Wissey (navigable to Stoke Ferry, 10 miles)	30	0
Denver Sluice (lock operating both ways)	31	1

Note: There is at present no through navigation between Castle Lock, 3 miles 5 furlongs below Bedford Bridge, and Tempsford.

River Little Ouse

Brandon Creek, junction with Ely Ouse, to:

Wilton Bridge	9	4
Brandon Staunch (boat rollers for light craft only)	13	3

River Cam

King's Mill, Cambridge, to:

Jesus Lock, Cambridge		6
Fen Ditton	3	4
Baitsbite Lock	4	5
Bottisham Lock	7	5
Upware, junction with Reach and Burwell Lodes. (Wicken Lode leads off Burwell Lode to Wicken Fen.)	11	2
Popes Corner (junction with Old West River)	14	3

CHAPTER NINE

Fenland Hire Cruising

The boating concerns on the Ouse have their own trading association listed at the back of the book, but this does not act as a booking agency. All concerns book direct, although some book also through agencies. There have been hire boats in the Cambridge area for very many years, and also on the Ouse in the Bedford, Huntingdon and Ely areas. Boats for hire originally were for the occasional fisherman, and pleasure rowing boats. As on the Thames, late Victorian days on the Cam were times of great punting activity by the undergraduates and their friends.

The earliest business to operate was H. C. Banham, who have occupied the Cambridge site where they are at present since 1906, and for two years beforehand from a site opposite the present marina. The business was built up by light craft manufactured on the premises, and there has been a tradition in this boatyard of building boats for the University Eights. The author has taken a Banham-built Canadian canoe for many hundreds of miles through the waterways, and it stood up very well to the many portages round derelict locks as only a well constructed boat could do. Mr Banham was the first to put motor launches on the river, and between the wars operated three passenger boats on the Cam. At present only hire cruisers are let out from the yard; these are very modern and even have central heating. Banham's also still let out on special charter the *Viscountess Bury,* the only one of three pleasure launches remaining, and the only one for hire anywhere on the Fens. This can accommodate a large party. The *Viscountess Bury* has been maintained in first class condition, although Banham's have had her since 1910. She was built in the 1880s on the Thames, was originally owned by the Ismay Electric Launch Company Ltd and was propelled by electricity. King Edward VII is reputed to have had several trips aboard this unique craft. For many years Banham's had a boatyard on the Broads at Horning, now part of H. T. Percival Ltd. This old family business gives remarkably good service, and in the traditional friendly way of the old boating family has helped to encourage other concerns on the river. After the war Harry Lincoln formed Appleyard Lincoln (Boatbuilders) at Ely, and commenced hiring boats. He was an old friend of H. C. Banham and it was a happy working arrangement.

Laurie Jones, after leaving the RAF, operated a hire fleet for some years at Huntingdon and is now located in a well-situated and managed marina at St Ives.

The old established concern of Childs & Hall at Huntingdon has been merged into the Elysian Hire Fleet, a well-known subsidiary of the Appleyard Lincoln (Boatbuilding) organisation.

The Fleming organisation started up at St Neots with two boats and doubtless in time other hire fleets will develop.

Hirers co-operate together on the Fens as they do on the Broads, and although hiring on the Fens is a small grouping they are certainly no poor relation. Fred Carrington's Fenland-built boats operate in Broadland hire fleets, and one of the Commissioners' inspection launches was built at Appleyard Lincoln's yard at Ely.

All boatyards issue brochures with data about the craft they hire, but in planning a cruise on the Fens consideration must be given to weather conditions, as at some periods of the year the Ouse locks have to be kept open for several days on end to enable water to be discharged from the upper reaches. Such conditions are exceptional, but it is worth watching for them. Similarly, of course, under certain high water conditions on the Broads craft can get temporarily marooned above Beccles Bridge and also above Potter Heigham. Usually in these circumstances the hire cruiser firm make arrangements to turn the boat round for the new hirer away from the yard.

There is at the time of writing only one hire organisation on the River Nene, Oundle Marina. This was started in recent years by Mr J. T. Newington, who has taken a very active interest in the river. A variety of craft are available for hire, including a small fleet of 2-6 berth cruisers. This concern has assisted greatly in making the Nene known to a wider selection of people.

CHAPTER TEN

The Detached Navigations of East Anglia

There are a number of short navigations in East Anglia of varying interest to the cruising enthusiast.

The River Glen

The Glen, a tributary of the Welland, is controlled by the Welland & Nene River Authority, and can only be entered when the tide makes a level through the tidal doors. The maximum beam of craft is 14ft 6in. There is usually a draught of from 2-3ft for 11½ miles. The Glen previously connected with Bourne Eau, which went to the town of Bourne. Surfleet, on the river, is a very pleasant village with a remarkable leaning church, the fourteenth century tower being 6ft out of centre, and an excellent inn opposite. The Glen is navigable to Tongue End, where there is a junction with the old Bourne Eau, running to the town of Bourne. Tongue End is about the only place that craft can turn above Pinchbeck Bars Bridge. A small cruiser could go above Tongue End, but the waterway is very narrow. Some maps incorrectly show a connection at Guthram Gowt with the old Black Sluice or South Forty Foot Drainage Navigation. This in fact is now closed and there never was any connection, as the levels are very different.

Above the Glen was the large Black Sluice navigable drain

running from near Guthram Gowt to Boston. Not connected with the Glen, its navigation is now completely closed. The River Glen has been straightened and made into a drainage river. So has the Witham, but on a much larger scale. There are numerous drainage cuts running into the Witham, but boatmen must be wary of entering these unknown streams as the sluices are automatically operated, depending upon the amount of water coming down the river. By far the most interesting of these northern rivers to the canal enthusiast is the area known as the Witham Navigable Drains. (The term 'drain', which occurs so often in Fenland, means a navigable canal, though its name does not necesarily bear any relation to its size. The Forty Foot Drain is not forty feet wide.) They are, however, outside the scope of this volume, although if you are cruising on the Witham they are well worth a visit.

The River Welland

The Welland was formerly navigable to Stamford. An Act to restore the navigation was passed as early as 1571, though the work was not completed until about 1665. More recently, its use declined, and it became a tidal navigation only, but in recent years a lock has been built at Fulney, a mile below Spalding Bridge; this allows a good deal of boating to take place in non-tidal water, and the Welland Sailing Club operates here. Now controlled by the Welland & Nene River Authority, this short navigation runs from the Wash inland as far as the Folly River Outfall above Crowland, a distance of 22 miles. There are no hire craft on the river and visitors should take the usual precautions in entering from the Wash.

Spalding is a fine old town with marked Dutch overtones, and is appropriately in that section of Lincolnshire called Holland. The time to visit Spalding is when the bulbs are out; then excursions are run from all over Britain to see the bulb fields. The river flows through the centre of the town, giving it a Dutch appearance. There are a number of very fine old buildings and a magnificent church, St Mary and St Nicholas, which dates from 1284.

The intrepid navigator who discovers the Welland can go upstream to about a mile from Crowland. This lies at the edge of Deeping Fen, and like all Fenland towns is on a little raised piece of land slightly higher than the swampy surrounding countryside. Crowland is famous for its great Benedictine Abbey, partly in ruins. The north aisle serves as a church for the parish, and this aisle and the tower are the only remains of the famous old abbey, but attached to them are magnificent ruins, the nave, the west arch of the central tower and other sections. In the town is the famous triangular bridge like none other in Britain. The waterway has been long gone, but has a curious bridge and its figures, alleged to have been taken from the abbey church, are reminders of a bygone Crowland.

The determined canoeist should under some circumstances be able to get to Stamford; certainly small craft that can be portaged can get well above the village of Market Deeping. The lock dimensions are 110ft by 30ft beam with a draught of 8ft to Spalding. Above Spalding the headroom is limited to just above 6ft, and the length of craft should not exceed 35ft.

The River Blyth

The River Blyth has long ceased to be a navigation except for a short tidal section from Blythburgh to the sea. It was made navigable by an Act pased in 1757; there were four locks, but these have long been closed. The river forms a refuge for sailing craft in inclement weather, but a short section is extremely pretty and worth a visit. There is a nature reserve by the tideway. The drainage authority is the East Suffolk & Norfolk River Authority. There is a Harbourmaster at Southwold, a small watering place with an unusual degree of charm. By-passed by the crowds, it remains a delightful place with a magnificent common running from the town towards the river, and a 500 year old church like a village cathedral. More unusual, Southwold still has its own brewery, which can be found for discerning lovers of the native beverage in certain corners of Broadland.

The River Alde

This river is known as the Ore below Orford. It starts to be navigable at Snape Bridge, passes Iken Cliff Inn and enters the North Sea at Shinglestreet. This is not a river for anyone but the expert. The entrance is the most difficult and dangerous in the Thames Estuary due to the shallowing shingle bar across the entrance. Even in quiet conditions there is usually a strong swell over the bar, while with any wind a dangerous sea is quickly raised. A pilot is essential with craft coming in and out. This is a tidal navigation and there are no restrictions on size imposed by entrance locks.

One mile south of Orford is Orfordness, one of the largest shingle spits in the country, long used as a research site by coastal physiographers. Here are excellent examples of shingle beach vegetation and several rare insects have been recorded. Havergate Island is famous for its colony of avocets which began breeding there in 1948. Colonies of Sandwich and Common Terns are among numerous other birds. During winter the lagoons are a refuge for large numbers of wildfowl and waders. A permit is required from the East Anglia Region of the Nature Conservancy for visiting Havergate Island and for some parts of Orfordness.

The Rivers Orwell and Gipping

The Orwell is an estuary leading up to Ipswich, famous for its bird life and the yachting around Pin Mill, a delightful spot but totally ruined by car invasion at weekends and holidays. There is a good waterside inn, the Butt & Oyster. You can sail up to the window at high tide and get your pint through it. Here you will see some old wooden sailing barges, the Webb family in the district being almost the last of the great army of barge builders and repairers.

Ipswich should really be a fine old town, but it has been so extensively modernised that it is difficult to find its ancient roots or its associations with Dickens. Its great virtue is the River Orwell, the only river in Suffolk which craft can use in virtually any tidal condition. Unfortunately, the Ipswich & Stowmarket Navigation, nearly 16 miles long with fifteen locks, was closed in 1934. The route is in a sorry state and no one has thought of reviving it, although the difficulties of doing so are not insurmountable. It would make a valuable amenity for Ipswich and the neighbourhood.

The River Stour

The River Stour, that beautiful river made famous by Constable and Gainsborough, has been a navigation since its Act of Parliament of 1705. However, the recent passing of an Act to allow the Essex River Authority to build a barrage at Brantham had the effect of blocking the navigation. There appeared to be no one to put up any effective opposition. The story of the River Stour and its lost navigation is a sad one, but it seems likely that the right of navigation by prescription still exists, and boat rollers have been constructed on the new barrage which will take a craft up to nearly 35ft long. Canoeing on the river is increasing and the river will probably become a haven for light craft, although some other obstructions have also been placed in it. To keep an eye on the present position, to develop the river and protect its amenities, and to check water abstraction, the River Stour Trust has been founded. The Trust is concerned with retaining the valley as a place of great beauty, and wants the towpath reopened to Sudbury.

The river is distinguished by a number of East Anglian mills of great charm, Wissington being a particularly fine example. The Trust encourages visitors to use the river in light craft.

Sudbury is an ancient 'wool town', though not ancient to look at, and it has continued weaving until the modern age. It was the Stour Navigation that did much for the town, enabling it to go ahead commercially faster than its competitors. Nayland is a charming village of pink-washed weavers' cottages and houses. Dedham and Flatford are familiar to everyone through Constable's paintings in which he featured barges in many of his pictures. The distances on the river are as follows:

Sudbury to:

	miles
Cornard Mill	1
Henny Street	2⅜
Pitmire Lock	3¾
Bures Mill	7⅜
Wormingford Mill	9
Nayland	12⅝
Boxted Mill	16⅛
Langham Weir	16⅝
Stratford St Mary Lock	19
Dedham Lock	20½
Flatford Lock	22⅛
Brantham Lock	23⅝
Cattawade Bridge	24⅜
Manningtree	25¾
Harwich Harbour	35¼

Chelmer & Blackwater Navigation

The Chelmer & Blackwater Navigation has the shallowest statutory draught of any navigation in the country, only 2ft. This navigation is the only one left in East Anglia operating through a number of locks. The Act to canalise the river to Chelmsford was passed in 1766. There were the usual objections from the town of Maldon, which opposed goods going inland by barge and, of course, considerable opposition from the millers who were always a problem to navigation promoters in East Anglia. There are thirteen locks and the distance to Chelmsford is 14 miles. John Rennie built Heybridge basin. The lock here is 107ft by 26ft by 12ft and there is no restriction on headroom. Dimensions to Chelmsford are 60ft by 16ft by 2ft with 6ft headroom. There are many fine willows along the banks and the navigation authority makes a lucrative business from selling these. Several very good mills mark the route. Chelmsford is a busy manufacturing town, very close to Marconi and his radio, with some old buildings and the old parish church elevated to cathedral status.

Useful Addresses

HIRING CONCERNS

(The number of boats and properties is liable to continuous alterations)

The Broads

Blakes (Norfolk Broads Holidays) Ltd; (Symbol 'A'),
Hoveton St John,
Wroxham, Norwich, NOR 41Z.
(Tel: Wroxham 2141)
(1130 boats, plus bungalows and chalets, etc.)

Hoseasons Sunshine Holidays Ltd; (Symbol 'Bluebird'),
Sunway House,
Oulton Broad,
Lowestoft.
(Tel: Lowestoft 62181) (850 boats and properties.)

Bradbeer Red Whale Fleet,
(Symbol 'Red Whale')
R. B. Bradbeer Ltd,
7 Battery Green Road,
Lowestoft.
(Tel: Lowestoft 3172/3) (250 boats and properties.)

Broads Holidays Ltd,
Port of Yarmouth Marina,
Caister Road,
Great Yarmouth.
(Tel: Great Yarmouth 56531) (Over 120 boats and properties.)

R. Moore & Sons Ltd,
Wroxham,
Norfolk.
(Tel: Wroxham 2293)

Waveney Yacht Station,
Burgh St Peter,
Beccles,
Suffolk.
(Tel: Aldeby 217)

There are a number of other independent concerns which book direct and these advertise frequently in *Motor Boat & Yachting* (fortnightly).

Hoseasons and Bradbeers book for craft on other English and Irish waterways. Boat Enquiries Ltd, of 12 Western Road, Oxford (tel: Oxford 48765/49097/45500) book holidays for the Broads, Fens, English canals as well as for Irish and foreign waterways.

For Organised Parties

Broads Tours Ltd,
Wroxham,
Norfolk, NOR 06Z.
(Tel: Wroxham 2207)

The Fens

P. Amos,
Hemingford Grey, Hunts.
(Tel: St Ives 3711) (Hires out rowing boats.)

H. C. Banham Ltd;
Pye-Banham Marina,
Cam Road,
Cambridge.
(Tel: Cambridge 59486/7) (2 to 6 berth cruisers.)

F. W. Carrington,
'Quiet Waters' Boatyard,
Earith,
Huntingdon.
(Tel. Earith 400) (2 to 6 berth cruisers)

Elysian Holidays Ltd;
Bridge Boatyard,
Huntingdon.
(Tel: Huntingdon 3060) (2 to 6 berth cruisers.)

Fleming Holidays Afloat Ltd;
St Neots Marina,
St Neots,
Hunts. (2 to 4 berth cruisers.)

L. H. Jones,
The Boathaven,
St Ives,
Hunts.
(Tel: St Ives 63463) (2 to 6 berth cruisers.)

Oundle Marina Ltd;
Oundle,
Northants.
(Tel: Oundle 3311) (2 to 6 berth cruisers.)

The Detached Navigations

On the River Stour there are boatyards hiring out light craft at the following places:

The Boathouse, Ballingdon Bridge,
Sudbury, Suffolk.

The Boathouse, Stratford St Mary,
Colchester, Essex.

The Boathouse, Dedham, Essex.

The Thatched Cottage, Flatford,
East Bergholt, Suffolk.

FACILITIES FOR THE PRIVATE OWNER

For the private owner seeking Broadland Marina facilities application should be made to the Hire firms, as many yards offer facilities for the private owner. These are too numerous to list, but but there are other concerns offering private mooring facilities, and these can be found by local enquiry.

On the Fens, the hire firms listed all offer facilities to the private ower and in addition facilities are available as follows:

Whitehouse Boatyard,
St Neots.
(Tel: St Neots 2763.)

Kelpie Marine,
Tempsford.
(Tel: Great Barford 249.)

A. R. Brearley,
St Neots Marina,
St Neots.
(Tel: St Neots 2411.)

Appleyard Lincoln (Boabuilders) Ltd;
Ely.
(Tel: Ely 2244/5.)

Hartford Marina,
Hartford.
(Tel: Huntingdon 4574.)

Buckden Marina,
Buckden.
(Tel: Buckden 355.)

A. V. Jackson (Boats) Ltd;
Stanground,
Peterborough.
(Tel. Peterborough 65933.)

W. Lee & Sons Ltd;
Stanground,
Peterborough.
(Tel: Peterborough 1792.)

A new marina is planned for Wyboston on the Great Ouse.

AUTHORITIES

The Broads
The Yarmouth Port & Haven Commissioners,
21 South Quay,
Great Yarmouth.
(Tel: Great Yarmouth 55151) (For bye-laws and registration.)

The Fens
The Welland & Nene River Authority,
Oundle,
Peterborough.
(Tel: Oundle 3366/7) (For bye-laws.)

Wisbech Town Council (port and pilotage authority),
Port Managing Offices,
Wisbech.
(Tel: Wisbech 5761/2125) (For pilotage enquiries.)

The Middle Level Commissioners,
Dartford Street,
March,
Cambridge.
(Tel: March 3232.)

(Lock-keeper—Stanground Northern Entrance, tel: Peterborough 66413.)
(Lock-keeper—Salter's Lode Southern Entrance, tel: Downham Market 2292.)

The Great Ouse River Authority,
Great Ouse House,
Clarendon Road,
Cambridge.
(Tel: Cambridge 61581) (For bye-laws and registration.)

The Kings Lynn Conservancy Board,
Harbour Office,
Common Staithe,
Kings Lynn. (Port authority: the harbourmaster may be able to arrange pilotage.)

The Detached Navigations
The Welland & Nene River Authority,
Oundle,
Peterborough.
(Tel: Oundle 3366/7.)

The Boston & Spalding Pilotage Authority,
Market Place,
Boston, Lincs. (Pilotage.)

Boston Corporation,
Harbourmaster.
(Tel: Boston 2328)
(Controls from below Boston Grand Sluice seawards.)

British Waterways Board
(controls Boston Grand Sluice and above on the Witham.)
Section Inspector (tel: Lincoln 20148).

The East Suffolk & Norfolk River Authority,
The Cedars,
Albemarle Road,
Norwich. NOR 81E.
(Tel: Norwich 53257/8.)

The Essex River Authority,
Rivers House,
Springfield Road,
Chelmsford, Essex.
(Tel: Chelmsford 57281.)

Chelmer & Blackwater Navigation Co Ltd;
Little Baddow,
Essex. (Tel: Danbury 2025).
Entrance Lock Heybridge (tel: Maldon 3506).

OTHER ADDRESSES

The Inland Waterways Association Ltd,
114 Regents Park Road,
London, NW1.
(Tel: 01-586-2556.)
(The Association publishes for 12½p an annual *Waterways Holiday Guide*. This lists firms who are members of the IWA and the facilities they offer. This information is usually the most up to date available.)

The Royal Yachting Association,
5 Buckingham Gate,
London SW1.
(Tel: 01-828-9296.)
(The RYA representative on the Yarmouth Port & Haven Commissioners is S. S. F. Horneor, Norfolk & Suffolk Yachting Association, Old Bank of England Court, Queen Street, Norwich, NOR 07J.)

The East Anglian Waterways Association Ltd,
Wych House,
St Ives,
Hunts.
(The East Anglian Waterways Association works closely with the Inland Waterways Association and the Great Ouse Restoration Society, and is linked with the Association of Nene River Clubs.)

The Nature Conservancy,
East Anglian Region,
60 Bracondale,
Norwich, NOR 58B.
(Tel: Norwich 20558) (Regional Officer: Dr M. George.)

Central Council for Physical Recreation,
Eastern Region,
5A Harpur Street,
Bedford.
(Tel: Bedford 50181.)

The Eastern Sports Council,
Secretary, L. J. Bridgeman,
Regional Officer c/o CCPR,
5A Harpur Street,
Bedford.
(Tel: Bedford 62191.)

(The Royal Yachting Association has a representative on the main council—R. H. Stevenson, 97 Newmarket Road, Norwich, NOR 23D. There is a Water Recreation Sub-committee and on this committee Mr Stevenson represents yachting, and Mr W. G. Undrill power boating. The East Anglian Waterways Association have their own representative, Mr J. Mayhead.)

British Canoe Union,
26/29 Park Crescent,
London W1.

Canoe Camping Club (affiliated to the BCU),
11 Lower Grosvenor Place,
London SW1.

The British Travel Authority,
64 St James's Street,
London SW1.
(Tel: 01-629-9191.)
(This authority has information about craft for hire and issues a booklet annually on Inland Waterways.)

The Broads

Norfolk & Suffolk Yachting Association,
Hon Secretary: M. H. Helliwell,
South Bank,
Wroxham,
Norwich, NOR 03Z.
(A grouping of 26 clubs, two clubs of which race during the winter.)

Norwich Rowing Committee,
Hon Secretary for entries: H. H. Scurfield.
Hon Secretary: E. J. Wright,
c/o Norwich Union Fire Insurance Society Ltd,
PO Box No 6,
Norwich, NOR 89A.

The Norfolk Naturalists Trust,
4 The Close, Norwich, NOR 16P.
(Tel: Norwich 25540.)

The Broads Society,
Hon Secretary: Miss Pamela Oakes,
63 Whitehall Road,
Norwich.

Broadland Youth Hostellers,
Martham Hostel (Youth Hostels Association),
Martham,
Great Yarmouth, Norfolk.

The Fens

The Great Ouse Boat Builders & Operators Association,
c/o F. W. Carrington,
Quiet Waters,
Earith, Hunts.
(This is the trade association for Ouse operators, but it does not act as a hire cruiser agency.)

Great Ouse Boating Association,
Hon Secretary: B. Robinson,
3 Elms Close,
Duxford,
Cambridge.

(This body includes some river clubs and also includes a representative of the traders on the river.)

Association of Nene River Clubs,
Hon Secretary: A. J. Hammond,
38 Fletton Avenue,
Peterborough.
(A federation of all the clubs on the river with The East Anglian Waterways Association; inter-affiliated.)

The Great Ouse Restoration Society,
Hon Secretary: D. J. Kettle,
8 Manor Close,
Kempston,
Bedford.

The Detached Navigations
The River Stour Trust,
Hon Secretary: Mrs P. E. Easton,
182 Temple Grove,
West Hanningfield,
Essex.

Further Reading

General

Seymour, John. *The Companion Guide to East Anglia* (Collins), 1970.

Turner, James. *Rivers of East Anglia* (Cassell), 1954.

(John Seymour is a cruising fan, and his general book contains an unusual amount of material about waterways suitable for boating.)

Broadland

Clark, R. *Black Sailed Traders* (David & Charles), 1971.

Davies, G. C. *Rivers and Broads of Norfolk and Suffolk* (Jarrold), 1883, and several other editions.

Day, J. Wentworth. *Portrait of the Broads* (Hale), 1967.

Broadland Adventure (Country Life), 1951.

Marshland Adventure (Harrap), 1950.

Norwich and the Broads (Batsford), 1953.

Dutt, W. A. *The Norfolk Broads* (Methuen), 1903.

Ellis, Dr E. A. *The Broads* (New Naturalist Series) (Collins), 1965.

Hamilton's Broads Charts and Handbook (Hamilton's Publications), yearly.

Hannaford, C. A., *The Charm of the Norfolk Broads* (Broads Tours Ltd), yearly.

Mottram, R. H. *The Broads* (Hale), 1952.

Suffling, Ernest R. *The Land of the Broads* (Benjamin Perry), 1892.

(The books by Davies, Dutt and Suffling, though long out of print, are not too difficult to buy secondhand, or they can be borrowed from a public library.)

In addition, Jarrolds publish yearly *What to Do on the Norfolk Broads* and Link House bring out *The Broads Book* yearly. Two publications of the Royal Geographical Society are of great interest: *The Origin of the Broads,* 1952, and *The Making of the Broads,* 1960. So is the Nature Conservancy's 1965 *Report on Broadland.*

Fenland

Astbury, A. K. *The Black Fens* (Golden Head Press), 1958.

B. B. *A Summer on the River Nene* (Kaye & Ward), 1967.

Bloom, Alan. *The Fens* (Hale, 1953.

Darby, H. C. *The Draining of the Fens* (Cambridge University Press), 1968.

Day, J. Wentworth. *The History of the Fens.*

Harris, L. E. *Vermuyden and the Fens* (Cleaver Hume Press), 1953.

Richards, M. E. *History of the Navigation of the Great Ouse ...between Bedford and St Ives* (Great Ouse Restoration Society), 1970.

Tibbs, Rodney. *Fenland River* (Terence Dalton), 1969.

Storey, E. *Portrait of the Fen Country* (Hale), 1971.

Miscellaneous

White, A. *Tideways and Byways in Essex and Suffolk* (Arnold), 1948.

The River Stour (Inland Waterways Association Ltd), 1966.

The East Anglian Waterways Association and The Broads Society produce regular journals which can be found in many libraries.

Acknowledgements

In many years of public work numerous people have been most helpful with information about East Anglia, much of which has been used in this volume. I should like to thank A. D. Truman Esq, chairman, and Christopher Groves Esq, of the Yarmouth Port & Haven Commissioners, and also Charles Collier Esq, who until his recent retirement (when Mr Groves succeeded him) was Chief Inspector of the Commissioners. James Hoseason Esq (Hoseason's Broadland Holidays) and Eric Mathew Esq (Red Whale Fleet) have been most helpful, as has Frank ('Jim') Brooker Esq, who retired recently after many years as managing director of Blakes (Norfolk Broads Holidays) Ltd, and S. Vincent Ellis Esq, clerk to the East Suffolk & Norfolk River Authority, and also Michael Helliwell Esq, Hon Sec, Norfolk & Suffolk Yachting Association.

My thanks are also due to the Welland & Nene River Authority, the Essex River Authority, the Great Ouse River Authority and the Middle Level Commissioners.

The Nature Conservancy in general and J. M. Scholfield Esq, the deputy regional officer (East Anglia) in particular, the Great Ouse Restoration Society, Leslie Critchley Esq, chairman of the East Anglian Waterways Association Ltd, the River Stour Trust, the National Trust, and the Association of River Nene Clubs have also been most helpful.

I would also like to thank L. C. ('Rex') Haylett Esq of Haylett & Porter for checking a number of items in the MS,

Acknowledgements

Geoffrey Dibb Esq for permission to mention a short section originally published in a slightly different form in *The Fens Book,* Dr E. A. Ellis for looking through my fauna and flora section and so generously allowing me to reproduce a short extract from his book, *The Broads,* and Charles Hadfield for his help with the MS.

The jacket photo and frontispiece is by courtesy of Blakes (Norfolk Broads Holidays) Ltd. The photo of Buckden Marina is reproduced by kind permission of Mr W. B. Carter of Buckden Marina. All the other photos were taken by the author.

The map of the Lower Ouse and river Nene is reproduced by kind permission of Messrs Imray, Norie Laurie & Wilson Ltd. The end map of the Broads needs one correction: the dyke to Catfield has been dredged out as well as Catfield Common Staithe.

In conclusion, may I thank the river patrol officers of the Yarmouth Port & Haven Commissioners for their help on numerous occasions and remind readers that these officers are there to help, and not just to enforce regulations.

LEWIS A. EDWARDS

Index

Index

Index